AL CAPONE—

The Hawk—Prohibition

Leon H. Tashjian

VANTAGE PRESS
New York/Los Angeles/Chicago

To my wife, Loretta

FIRST EDITION

Copyright © 1989 by Leon H. Tashjian

Published by Vantage Press, Inc.
516 West 34th Street, New York, New York 10001
Manufactured in the United States of America
ISBN: 0-533-08095-9

Library of Congress Catalog No.: 88-90230

Contents

Introduction

THIS IS A TRUE story, "my story," covering the infamous Prohibition era in Chicago and the corruption and power struggle that—even to the present day—has never been duplicated in any American city. My story includes events that occurred during the 1920s when Prohibition was at its peak, as well as follow-up stories that occurred during the thirties and forties.

At twenty-nine years of age, I was the youngest United States Deputy Marshal. President Calvin Coolidge issued me a bench warrant to subpoena and arrest several dangerous criminals—to bring them in DEAD OR ALIVE. The president of the United States selected me as sergeant of arms in unseating Frank L. Smith, the United States senator, regarding the slush fund board. I also worked on narcotic cases, bucket shops, and other matters too numerous to mention here; some of these are covered in my story.

The stories and cases, as told in this book, are 100 percent true. I was known to many as "the Hawk."

The Early Years:
Life on the Street

A KID LIVING ON the streets of Chicago, twelve years old. Me. A street kid. A runaway. My good parents would writhe in their graves, God bless 'em, to hear me talk about it, but it's true. They had their pride, you know. But I did what I had to do.

Now, there's an art to living on the streets. It was high adventure for a young boy. In 1908, Chicago was one helluva town.

My family were still in New York, where I was born. They didn't even know where I was. They were a moneyed family, understand; I didn't have to live on the streets. But when I look at it now, it was because they were moneyed that I had to get out on my own. At twelve I figured I was a man; I could make it on my own. Just a smartass kid itching to take the world by the tail. And damned if I didn't do it.

It seems like fate takes a peculiar delight in irony, and having me be born into a family of means was one of the great ironies. I am a person not meant to be coddled and protected in the world. I'm an adventurer, an independent, a maverick. I'd rather have a challenge; I'd rather have it made hard for me so I can rise to the occasion and prove my mettle. I'd rather have it that way than have it made easy. Easy Street just wasn't my style. Not then. Not as a kid.

Course it's different now. I like having means now, you bet your bippy I do; it's comfortable. But the thing

1

that makes it good is that they are my own means. I made it on my own. Nobody gave me anything.

I guess I've always had this stubborn streak of wanting to do things my own way. That's what life is all about, if you ask me. Doing it your own way. Digging down inside yourself to find your own strength and using that strength and your own talents to meet a challenge. And all that paid off later in my life. Moments when I was face to face with Al Capone, Yellow Kid Weil, Dago Mangano.

My father, too, was a man of his own mind. He lived a courageous life himself; maybe that's why he understood when I left. Although I didn't know it then, I had to take my chances. It was like jumping off a cliff. Maybe my parents would never forgive me; maybe they would never speak to me again. But I had to do what I had to do.

My boyhood up to the time I left had been pretty pleasant, I won't deny that. My parents were good people and they provided very well for us, my brother and sister and myself. Quite a bit above average, in fact.

My father and mother had come to America before the turn of the century; 1894 it was. Gave up everything they had in Turkey, because of religious persecution, and went to Jerusalem. Then they gave up everything again and came to America. Like thousands, hundreds of thousands of refugees, adventurers, and dreamers—people stripped of their human rights in other lands—my parents arrived at Ellis Island with pockets empty of everything but hope.

These are the people who made America. People with the courage to leave their homeland and put down roots in a new land and build a new and better country. My father and mother were part of that tradition, part of that dream, part of the history of America.

Originally they were from Sivas, Turkey, both of them. They were married there. They were both titled nobility in the old Armenian circles, but the Turks, who had taken over by then, didn't recognize Armenian ways or titles or anything. If the old ways had prevailed, my brother and I would be *beys* and my younger sister a princess. But all that gave way long ago.

My father, denied his place in Armenian royalty when the Turks took over his country, had made himself a very important man in the Oriental rug business in Constantinople. But he was a very religious man. And he suffered for that at the hands of the Turks, who were not Christian. They persecuted Christians.

So my mother and father, John and Acoby Tashjian, just recently married and young and courageous, fled from the persecution in Turkey and went to Jerusalem. My father spoke and read fourteen languages, so he could get by very well in any major center of the world. He had faith in himself, that he could set himself up anywhere and do business with many peoples of the world. And he did.

Now, while he was in Jerusalem and very active in the religious circles of the Armenian community there, he became a preacher and had a certain tattoo put on, reaching up onto one hand between his thumb and first finger. I remember that tattoo because it always fascinated me as a boy; it seemed very dramatic to me, very mysterious. A mark from a distant life. My father had this strange, odd-shape, indistinct-form mark, and it would be with him forever.

My older brother, Vaharm, was born to them on the way over, right there on the boat. That was 1894. Two years later I was born in New York City, where my father was struggling with his English and building up a big business. My father had arrived in America with nothing but his brains, what he had in his head about Oriental rugs and tapestries and antiques, and the foreign languages he spoke. It was hard for him because English was not one of his better languages. He could speak it, but it was always very difficult to understand him.

But he got by. Determination makes up for a lot of things. And in a few years he built up a substantial business in New York City and became known as the King of Oriental Rugs. The Turks could refuse to recognize his title of Armenian royalty in the old country, but they couldn't stop my father from creating a new title for himself in the new country. King of Oriental Rugs. And that was a matter of pride for him, and rightly so, for my father had come to America with nothing and had built something out of his own mind and his own hard work.

But that was his destiny, not mine. No way was I going to become any Prince of Oriental Rugs!

I look back now and I can honestly say I was happy enough as a kid. Good parents, nice house, nice clothes, all that sort of thing. Except for one problem. I felt suffocated. Chrissake, I had maids to dress me! We wore knickers in those days, those knee pants with the knee high socks. And shirts and ties, which is an inhuman thing to do to a kid. My family's maid would lay out these fancy dan clothes for me and help me get dressed—you can bet I wasn't going to stand for that very long! I may have been smaller than a lot of my pals, but I was no sissy! I would've liked to have hung the whole houseful of maids by their hair! If I had stayed home much longer, I just might've. But I thought of a better plan.

I saved up a little money of my own, secretly, and just walked away one day. Just walked out of the house and didn't look back. Didn't even say good-bye. Bought me a ticket on the train to Chicago. One way. Boy, did I feel like big stuff.

First thing I did when I arrived in Chicago, which was to be the only city I ever really loved in my life, was scout around. I saw some boys about my age selling papers on the street, so I asked some questions. How'd they get that job? At first they were pretty tight-lipped, afraid I might be being paid to get something on them. I learned soon enough to be that way too because some of the things they did, which pretty soon I was doing too, were not exactly legal. But I stuck around and talked tough like them, and I listened to what they said and tried to put the pieces together and form a plan.

Now, these kids were tough. I could tell they knew what they were doing. They were shrewd; they were nobody's dummies. And I wanted to know what they knew.

So I hung around and pretty soon I got their trust, and they began to tell me the ins and outs of living on the street. And they showed me the places they had learned to use for survival. I started hanging around with them and adopted some of their ways and added some ways of my own. And my life on the street was off and running.

Off and running—I wish I had a nickel for every time we were off and running! Running away from somebody or other chasing us because we were selling stolen—or yesterday's papers, or because we had stuffed our pockets full of food that we weren't entitled to. Or because we slept where people weren't supposed to sleep. But it was a life. An exhilarating primitive life, a life of survival in the jungle. It was a high old time of a cocky little kid from New York.

Chicago, 1908. Me, a skinny kid scraping a living off the streets. First, I elbowed my way into the newsboy business. What I learned was the some of the newsboys selling papers on the street were doing it legitimately, and others were not. If you did it legitimately, you had to turn in some of the money to the *Daily News's* office, Now, even though I was twelve, I was a small kid and I looked only about nine or ten. They might give a twelve-year-old a job in those days, better a fourteen-year-old. But a nine-year-old, no way. So I did what some of the other kids did.

About four o'clock in the morning we would lie in wait for the *Daily News's* trucks, which came around and dropped off the packages of papers for the legitimate newsboys. Soon as the truck rounded the corner we'd dart out from the shadows and grab some of the papers and run. And then we'd go sell 'em on the street corners and in the saloons.

There was a certain saloon that we hung out in that was essential to our survival. The Hanna and Hoag Saloon. I'll never forget it. Out front they had cement statues of the two owners, big as life. Those statues used to strike us funny and we'd run up to them and bow and carry on some nonsense conversations. But those guys were our benefactors, whether they knew it or not.

Now, inside the saloon they had a gentleman who presided grandly over the proceedings, all dressed up in a white top hat, white shirt, black slacks, and a black bow tie. A very elegant fellow for a saloon.

We'd go in there, me and my pals, to sell our papers. Maybe it was the papers we had grabbed from the drop-off points or maybe it was papers we picked up in the alleys where the trucks dumped the old one from yesterday, papers that were going to be thrown away. Either way we rationalized that they had extra papers, more papers than they needed. Even yesterday's news was almost up to date, we figured. We didn't want to think of ourselves as thieves or hoodlums, y' know; we were just kids trying to get by in a crazy world.

So we'd go in there, arrogant little cusses, acting like we owned the place; and we'd call out, "Extra! Extra! Read

6

all about it!" And we'd mingle in and out among the customers and sell a few papers and work our way down to the end where they had the food. The customers could buy a beer for a nickel in those days or whiskey for fifteen cents. And with their drink they could get a nice big sandwich, ham or roast beef, maybe dipped in hot juice, with cheese on it, whatever they wanted. "Free lunch," they called it. All this for a nickel beer.

Well, we'd work our way down to the end where the food was, selling our day-old or our copped papers, and when we got down there we'd just help ourselves to the free lunch. The man in the white hat and bow tie would sort of overlook us; maybe he didn't want to be seen bullying the newsboys or maybe he figured it was good to have us around, that it was a convenience to the customers if they could buy their papers in there. We just avoided his look, and we'd grab handfuls of food and stuff it in our pockets when we thought he wasn't looking; then on a given signal we'd grab a couple of more handfuls and hightail it outa there before anybody caught on to our shenanigans about the papers.

We'd run out into the alley, scared to death we were being chased, and when we finally ran out of breath we'd look back and our pursuers were always only in our minds. We'd laugh with relief, and we'd sit down and divvy up our take. Pretty damn good lunch. And the price was right.

Now, a lot of the people went for the free lunch. But I had two pals in particular. The three of us hung around together; we made quite a team. We had the free-lunch routine down to a science. It was a matter of timing—get in; sell some papers; coordinate our move over to the food; grab some bread, some meat, some cheese; and hightail it outa there. We were hot.

The alley we went to—well, the alley was our home.

We ate there, we slept there, and we got most of our papers there. At night we'd stack up some of the leftover papers and sleep on them. Or sometimes we'd build a little shack, a primitive sort of lean-to, out of cardboard or tar paper or whatever we could find. When it was really cold, when winter came, we did something riskier. We'd climb up into the back end of the newspaper trucks that were parked overnight in the alley and sleep inside the trucks.

The newspaper men came so early in the morning, before it got light, that we had to sleep with one eye open in order not to get caught. But we trained ourselves to hear 'em coming. We'd scramble out the back end of those trucks in a flash, not even awake yet, just throwing our survival instinct into gear, and we'd disappear down the alley, some guy shakin' his fist at us. But they never caught us. We were quick as jackrabbits and they didn't have the time to take out after us.

First thing we'd do in the morning was go and clean up for the day. We had two places to do that. We could wait around for the saloons to open up and go in there and use their washroom. Splash our faces; run wet hands through our hair. Or we could go to the YMCA. If the YMCA knew you had no home, they'd let you go in, and they'd give you a towel and soap so you could take a bath. It was free. We made an art out of finding the free stuff.

The alley we used was called the *Daily News* Alley, in between Lasalle and Wells streets. It's still there today. It's behind the place where they print the Chicago *Daily News*. Down the alley there used to be a little stand where you could buy hot dogs. We called 'em red hots. For three cents they'd give you a hot dog and a bun. And lemonade for a penny. We lived on that; that was our dinner. Four cents.

Now, when you live on the street, it isn't like you have a nice wardrobe closet somewhere. You just have one set of clothes, the clothes on your back. You just live on foot, like a gypsy or a bedouin or something; it's a way of life. Unrooted. So our clothes took a pretty tough beating. We slept in 'em; we wore 'em around the clock, day in, day out. Take my word for it, they would get pretty bad. So we had to replace 'em sometimes.

Now, down on South Water Street they had special sales from time to time, and everything would be out on the sidewalk in big pushcarts. Lots of crowds, everybody jamming around to paw over the goods.

We'd go over there and we'd have one guy stir up some mischief or ask a bunch of questions and tie up the storekeeper's attention. Then the other two guys would grab a couple of things—a jacket, a pair of pants, a handful of shirts that could be stuffed inside our coats—and we'd take off. Then we'd go to another place and do the same, until each guy had what he needed.

A little petty thievery, learning to scramble in the world. Sure, it was exciting for a while to live by our wits. But I think what we learned is that there's no real payoff in it. There's no progress. A few months of scrambling and we weren't any better off than we were when we started. And you can't go through life like that. Sleeping in the back of a truck, selling yesterday's papers, eating hot dogs every night. How many hot dogs can you eat before you gag on 'em.

But all this wisdom did not appear to us for quite a while. Me, probably the stubbornest and the most ambitious among us, I was trying hard to beat the system. While the other guys settled for the newsboy life, legitimate or not, I went and got two other jobs. And continued to sell papers, too. First, I lined up a job running Western Union telegrams. Everything was by foot then. There were horses and carriages, of course, but not for a messenger job like that.

It started with a conversation with a man in the saloon.

9

I heard him say something about not being able to depend on the kids who were running his telegrams for him. So I spoke up. Told him I could run like a jackrabbit and I was very reliable. And the man gave me a trial.

You had to deliver each telegram personally, and there was no way to do it but on foot. Sometimes it would be miles. They paid so much per telegram, so the more you hustled the more money you made. Well, I accepted the challenge and the man took a liking to me, so I made a few bucks that way.

Then I also took on a shoeshine job. There was a shoeshine parlor on the street corner, an inside place, real nice. They didn't care about my age. Far as they were concerned they could get away with paying a kid less than a regular worker, even though I did just as good a job. Matter of fact, I did one helluva job, I was so determined to make those shoes shine like mirrors. A shoeshine was five cents, a cent of which was mine. Same pay I got for the papers, which sold for two pennies in those days.

Now, this experience was more valuable than it seemed. Years later I went into the shoeshine business myself. Had a shop of my own, took on a partner, and later sold off the business at a nice profit. More than that, the shoeshine parlor in those days was a place where everybody met and kicked around the issues of the day, political matters, public controversies. And as it turned out, my shoeshine parlor was the arena where I made my first political contacts.

After about a year of proving that I could survive on my own, and proving too that there wasn't much future in scraping a living off the streets, something happened that was almost too much for me to believe.

Now, I had been sellin' papers for a long time. I liked to follow the front-page news, y' know, keep up on what

10

was going on in the world, local politics and such. But I didn't, as a general rule, read past the first page. Except for the funnies.

Me and my pals, we'd lounge around in the newsboys' alley and read the funnies, when we didn't have anything else to do. We acted real casual about it, actin' like we liked living there. We'd just sit down in the alley by the big trash cans and stretch our feet and lean against the building and page through the paper. I guess we fantasized that we were successful businessmen putting our feet up in some fancy living room somewhere. Tryin' it on for size, the good life. And to tell you the truth, it felt a lot better than the way we were living. I can say that now, but not a one of us would have admitted to it then.

So on one particular day I was paging through the paper more thoroughly than usual, uncharacteristically of me, and what jumped out of the pages and hit me right in the face—an ad for a grand opening of a new store, run by the King of Oriental Rugs! Now, that made me mad! Nobody, I thought, had better be using that name except my father! And sure enough, there was his name, right there at the bottom of the ad—John Tashjian.

I knew instantly it was my folk's way of finding me. I knew that somehow they had gotten some scraps of information from my old cronies in New York that if I went anywhere it would be Chicago. They must've already tried to track me down and ended up on dead-end streets and decided their best shot was Chicago. Moved all the way from New York in search of their prodigal son.

Now, at that point maybe some guys would be afraid. Afraid to go home, afraid of what their family would say. Or do. I didn't say a word to my buddies. I just tore out the part of the ad with the address on it and stuck it in my pocket. No other information went in my pocket. And I was the only one in the world who knew what the scrap of paper and address were for.

I pushed it around in my mind for a long time, the idea about my parents. Chewed on it night and day. Looked at the ad when I was feelin' good and when I was feelin' down. And my folks began to haunt me. They were with me everywhere I went. I knew that my good mother would be having a hard time nursing a broken heart as long as her son was gone. And my father. Well, he would be very protective of her. And even if he understood what had made me run away and go off on my own, he would want me to come back and heal my mother's sadness.

I tried to push them out of my mind. At least out to the edges, in the shadows. But I kept seeing their faces. The sad eyes of my mother. She didn't deserve what I had done. Walked out on my family. They were good people. And the stern eyes of my father. I knew he expected me to be responsible for my actions. And running away, disappearing forever, was not anybody's idea of responsible.

I looked for that ad in a lot of papers. And every time I found it I felt their love for me, reaching right out of the paper. Sometimes I threw away my crumpled up piece of newspaper with the address on it and replaced it with a new scrap of paper with the same information. I had the address long since memorized. I just wanted to have it with me.

Finally, one day, real early in the morning, I got myself all spiffied up and took off. My pals didn't think anything of it, just thought I was going to take care of my various part-time jobs, my street-life ritual. I didn't know what I was going to do, I just knew I was going to try something.

I went to the store whose address I had kept stuffed in my pocket for weeks now. Funny how hard my heart was beating when I got within a few blocks of the place. Now, you've got to understand, I was a pretty tough young whippersnapper by this time. Been living off the streets for nearly a year. I was just a kid, but I was already an old man in ways. Street wise. Tough. I was sure I was a man, had proved my manhood and done a good job of it, too. Hadn't I survived without anybody's help? Found me three different jobs, just like a man, and held them down? Sellin' papers, shinin' folks' shoes, delivering telegrams for Western Union? I was tough all right. Never complained about hunger or cold, never asked anybody for a favor, just got out there in the jungle of a city and made my own way. Isn't that the way my father had done it? Well, not exactly.

I didn't go too near the store. I wasn't ready to really go through with this thing yet. I cased out the place. Watched. Day after day. I was gettin' a free shower at the YMCA and washin' out my clothes in the YMCA sink and tryin' to make a nice appearance every day. Just in case I decided to go to my father's store. And just in case I saw my father.

Then one day I did. I saw my father. A good man, my father was. A nice-looking gentleman. Even if he had not been such a handsome figure of a man, he was my father. It felt good to see him.

I went back to the newsboys' alley that night. Didn't say a word. Never had said a word about my trips or my sudden concern with my appearance. It was quite a trick to look reasonably clean, considering our circumstances there. My buddies began to razz me about puttin' on airs, but I just said it helped me get more shoeshines and bigger tips when I delivered a telegram. They bought that.

But everything had changed for me. Though not on the outside. I still kept on making my rounds, doing my jobs. But inside me things had changed. The jig was up.

The heart of the adventure had been sucked away—by a newspaper ad.

I knew I would go home. I didn't know when, but I felt it like ropes tugging on me, and I knew that I was finished fighting their pull. It was okay now, I thought. It was okay to go home.

One day I watched for my father to leave the store. I was all dressed up, about as clean as I could get. Wanted to look like a nice young man so the people who worked in the store wouldn't think about me too much. Wouldn't particularly notice me, y' know.

So I walked right into my father's store. Walked right up to a man who seemed to be in charge and started to ask questions about having an oriental rug cleaned. I knew the right questions to ask. Been raised around rugs all my life. Said I was asking for my mother.

While I was in there, I tried to get some more information, like where my parents lived. I couldn't ask right out, but I looked around the desk for something that would tell me what I wanted to know. No soap.

I was getting nervous about being there, afraid my father would come back. They kept asking me more questions than I wanted to answer, and I was getting antsy. I left. And I snuck down the street like a hunted animal. What was I to do? I found their address so I went home, my father and mother were happy to see me. I finished school, graduated from High School, found a job until we entered World War One. Enlisted and discharged when Armistice was signed. I came home again. After a few weeks looked for work. Filed an application for Internal Revenue Deputy Agent, was hired but no action went into being a United States Deputy Marshall for many years. Resigned and entered Politics.

Day of the Hawk: The Man Who Brought in Capone

THE HAWK. I WAS called the Hawk because I always seized my prey. Never once failed to bring in my man. The youngest United States deputy marshal and the only one with that record. Never once failed to return a writ without my man. No matter how elusive he was, how ruthless or desperate, it was known I wouldn't quit. I'd get my man.

Me, a little guy weighing in at a hundred-thirty pounds. Up against the notorious gangsters of the Prohibition Era in Chicago. Dillinger, Yellow Kid Weil, Terry Druggan, Frankie Lake, and Dago Mangano. I still have a scar on my leg from Mangano's bullet. Even the great Al Capone. I was the guy who first brought in Capone. Mountain of a man. In more ways than one.

It cost me a lot. I was shot, my family was threatened, my wife lost a child and her hair turned white. And I was framed. A national scandal was organized to try and get me out of the picture. My career never recovered from that. Today I look back at my life and it's as clear as it was sixty, seventy years ago. The faces, the names, the dates. Etched in my bones, every one of them.

Capone, always the gentleman. Dressed elegantly but always understated. They make a monster out of him now—and he wasn't. He was a kind man. It was his men who were monsters. He was behind them, of course. But

15

to deal with Mr. Capone himself, he was a gentleman. Oh, they did some dirty work all right. But the big man himself never even carried a gun. That's why it was so hard for the government to ever get anything on him. But one thing was to be said for him, Al Capone did more for the poor during the hard times than all the government agencies put together. People don't know that anymore, but it's true.

Oh, I knew 'em all. And what a colorful time it was. Diamond Joe Esposito, with diamonds on his vest. What a showman. Dago Lawrence Mangano. Now, there was a nice fella. Just looking to make a buck on Prohibition. And that crazy Terry Druggan. Kiss of death. He's the one I wish I'd never met.

I close my eyes and—I don't even have to close my eyes. It's there, waiting for me. I can even smell it. The streets of Chicago, Prohibition, gunfire. The secret distilleries, roadhouses, speakeasies. That time will never come again. What an era. And I was a part of it. Right in the thick of it. All over the papers. I was always in the papers. Got books of clippings. People love my books of clippings. People long for a time of such glamour, such color. The excitement. The danger. Oh, it was a time. And it will never come again.

I'm turning ninety-two years young soon. Spry as a jackrabbit. And my Babe, she's still pretty as a picture at eighty-five. We look back now and we remember it all. Finally, the clouds have settled. Finally, we can talk about it.

Capone

FIRST TIME I EVER saw Capone he was expecting me, y' see. Somehow those people had ways of knowing things. Far as we could figure, he had not and could not possibly have penetrated the federal government's information flow, but somehow he knew. Now, I'm just telling you what I sensed; there wasn't ever anything said. Not by him, not by his men. It was in the air. A sort of invisible welcome mat. Only not a friendly one.

It was out in Stickney, Illinois, where I tracked him down. Now, I didn't know for sure I could get him there, but from the most reliable information I could get, it was my best shot.

Stickney was a pretty place, green hills and tall trees, about forty, fifty miles outside the city of Chicago. I had a subpoena for Mr. Capone to make an appearance in court. Just answer some questions about violations of the Volstead Act, about the selling of barrels of beer and certain quantities of alcohol. That was all illegal in those days, anything to do with the sale of alcohol.

While the boys were over in Europe fighting the war—the big one, y' know, World War One, the war we really believed would be the end of all wars—well, that was when these ladies up in Evanston took advantage of our fighting boys—all our boys, millions of 'em, being overseas, fighting for our country, not being around to vote. Those ladies put their temperance issue on the ballot and got it passed, what with all the fighting men gone. Now, if there

17

had been a fair representation of public opinion, there's no way that bill would ever have been passed. But the boys came home to that. No beer, no whiskey, no alcohol of any kind. Welcome home, boys; by the way, we had a vote while you were gone.

Anyway, I had this subpoena to deliver to Mr. Capone. Now, I knew of him, of course; everybody knew of Al Capone. Chrissake, he owned the city of Chicago. But you almost never heard of anybody seeing him. Not that he was a recluse or anything like that. In fact he was a high liver, as they say. He just never flaunted anything. I mean he never called attention to himself. He did what he did, he went where he went, and maybe you'd see his cars go by and you'd wonder, maybe that's Mr. Capone.

I say cars because he never traveled alone. Had a big car for himself, chauffeured, of course, with his men right beside him. And there was always a car ahead of him and another car behind him. Like a wall around him. Bullet-proof glass and everything. Matter of fact, it was said the man never carried a gun himself. Never carried a weapon of any kind. Didn't need to, y' know, what with his lieu-tenants around him all the time. Far as I know, he never even had a penknife.

His lieutenants were his weapons. They were his alter ego, like an extension of himself. He never did the dirty work himself. Didn't have to. That's a lot of why it was so hard to ever get anything on him. Nobody really knew who was around Capone, he had so many men, and their names were not necessarily real names at all. One thing we did know was that when his own men wanted to contact him, call him or something, they had to go by a number instead of a name. He had all his men numbered, and then he would change the numbers from time to time. Kept their anonymity that way, just in case the line was being

18

tapped or they were being watched. And then he kept his own hands clean. At least for appearances.

The United States district attorney's office had issued the subpoena. Bring in Al Capone. They gave it to the Hawk, y' know, because they wanted to be sure Capone wouldn't slip through anybody's fingers. They knew if anybody could bring him in, I was the one. I had that reputation to keep up. I'd stick to it, come hell or high water, till I brought him in, no matter who they sent me out after. I'd bring him in or die trying.

So I drove up to Stickney, Illinois, in my black Wills Saint Claire, with my United States deputy marshal emblem beside the license plate in the front and my siren. That was a special car; I had the only one with an emblem on the front. I have to say, though, sometimes it got in the way. I couldn't drive up to deliver a subpoena with that emblem like a red flag announcing my coming. Y' see, if it's known you represent the federal government, well, the people you're after disappear.

You have to sneak up on them; that's the art of it. The risk of them disappearing is the easy part. The real danger is when they do confront you. With a weapon. The trick is to corner your man, without his knowing who you are; get him to acknowledge his identity, usually in some sneaky way; and then quick announce the purpose of your visit, all before he realizes what you're up to. If you can get that far, you have a pretty good chance that he'll think twice before he decides to mess up a United States deputy marshal. Still, he might try; you never know.

So it was in a big house, Capone's operation. Looked like a home, a very elegant home. But inside they had illegal gambling and drinking going on. It was what was known in those days as a roadhouse. I parked quite a distance away and walked, so as not to announce myself too clearly, y' know. Just strolled up to the place like I was just dropping in to gamble a little or have a drink.

I went inside, acting like I was a regular, just cool, nothing to notice, y' know. I was trying to get a quick survey of what was going on—slot machines operating very heavily all along the walls, gambling going on at tables in the room, huge bar along the one wall. I had barely got an impression when out of nowhere I was surrounded by a circle of men, ten or twelve of 'em, holding guns on me. Out of nowhere. It was like a magic trick or something. I'll never be able to figure out how they did that. I'm a very alert guy, always have been. Not much goes by me, I can assure you. And yet these ten, twelve armed men materialized in an instant, just like that. It was like they were part of the wall and just suddenly came to life. Like the wall came alive.

They made a circle around me, these ten or twelve men. Waiting. Just waiting. Like statues. Waiting for me to do something. I froze, these guns staring at me.

"Afternoon, gentlemen," I said.

They didn't move. Didn't bat an eye.

"I'd like to see Mr. Capone."

One of them recognized me. Nobody I knew, y' understand, but there was no doubt at all that he knew me. Well, my picture had been in the papers quite a bit. That was all very nice, made me feel good, y' know, but there were moments when I wished there wasn't any such thing as a newspaper. This was one of those moments.

"Go back. Go back," this guy said. "Go to where you're supposed to be. Forget it."

I didn't know if he was speaking to me or not. If it was to me, I wasn't sure how I was going to play this. But the other guys disappeared as quick as they had magically appeared.

"He's upstairs," the one guy said to me. "Go on up and see him."

"Thank you very kindly," I said. And without looking back I went up to the second floor, by the staircase that was there.

I got to the top of the stairs and there were several doors to choose from. Nobody there to escort me or anything. That seemed odd to me. Gave me a feeling I was being watched by somebody I couldn't see.

Through an open door I could see a huge room with a high-quality, Oriental rug; it looked real elegant. Now, you're talking to an Armenian who knows Oriental rugs. My father was one of the most knowledgeable men in the business of Oriental rugs and tapestries and antiques. I grew up with all that. And this was a high-quality, Oriental rug, and the furniture was expensive.

I walked right in. And it looked to me like the man was expecting me. The others must have given him signals that somebody was coming up. That's the way they operate. You don't see the signals; it's like they're invisible signals. But they know.

"Mr. Capone?" I asked him.

He was sitting in a red velvet, upholstered, high-back chair over by the window, a little table beside him. He didn't nod or anything; he just sat there watching me.

Now, part of the procedure was to get him to acknowledge his identity. And he wasn't. *Well*, I thought, *I just have to go for it.*

"I'm Lee Tashjian, Mr. Capone. United States deputy marshal."

He just sat there. Glanced down at his hands in his lap. Then slowly he looked up, his eyes boring into mine. "What can I do for you, Mr. Tashjian?"

Very polite. And I have to tell you, in all the dealings

21

I ever had with this man, he was always the picture of a gentleman.

I flashed him my identification card and reached up and turned my lapel underside out to show my badge. "United States deputy marshal," I said again. He nodded. Never took his eyes off me. He didn't even blink, I swear it.

"I have a subpoena for you, Mr. Capone."

"Okay," he said. "I'll have a look at that subpoena, Mr. Tashjian. If that's agreeable to you."

He glanced at his fingernails. Sort of rubbed them, like he wanted to be sure they looked nice. Properly manicured and all. It was a study in casualness, like he wasn't fazed by the subpoena.

Now remember, you have to understand, this was the first time that anyone representing the federal government had ever delivered a subpoena on Al Capone. I knew that inside he must be damn angry; he had to be. But you couldn't tell it. And I began to wonder. Why was he so cocksure of himself? We had him on something. I had no way of knowing exactly what the charges were or just what the government wanted to question him about; that was not my job. My job was to find him, corner him, get him to acknowledge his identity, and then officially deliver the subpoena. But it began to look like he knew more about this than I did. Here he was, all dressed up like he was going to Sunday church service, not a hair out of place or a wrinkle in his expensive suit; and I was delivering a subpoena on him from the United States government, and the man never twitched a muscle. Just sat there looking at his fingernails. Like he thought I was just a mosquito in the room, who would soon buzz off.

I walked over and held out the subpoena. He looked

me right in the eye, reaching out, sort of in slow motion. "Thank you, Mr. Tashjian," he said. Smiling. Thank you. Now, no one had ever thanked me before for delivering a government subpoena on him. It made me want to laugh. But I thought it was not really advisable at that moment.

Capone took the subpoena and unfolded it, slowly, carefully. Like it was brittle parchment and might crack. I just watched. He was a very large man. Huskily built. Well over two hundred pounds, no doubt of it. And I was standing there, a hundred thirty pounds and a badge. Course I had a gun, my Smith and Wesson 45, in a shoulder holster. I didn't know then that Capone was never armed. I had to assume he was.

Now, I was standing there staring at an excellent-looking gentleman. Around six feet tall, maybe a little under, a good, hefty two hundred fifty pounds at least. And the man was immaculate from head to foot. Groomed like he had just stepped out of a gentlemen's magazine. His suit had to have cost a fortune, was specially tailored for him obviously. I have to say, however, that he was not a physically fit man. He was mostly stomach. Nor a very agile man, being so husky. And that particular point was in my favor. Me, I was quick. Agile as a jackrabbit. Always have been.

I looked closely while Capone read the subpoena to himself. He was a soft-shaven man, showing a scar on his cheek. Sleek black hair, a little wispy around the edges, was growing thin. Definitely growing thin. He was probably in his middle forties, I figured.

Now, this suit of his was expensive, but it wasn't flashy. Very understated, in fact. Like he didn't want to be noticed. Out in public, if you didn't know his face, you wouldn't think much about him being anybody special. A man of

23

money, maybe, to dress with that kind of quality, but not a flamboyant man. Not showy.

"Okay," he now said, "I'll answer the subpoena. With my attorneys."

"Okay, Mr. Capone. That takes care of the purpose of my visit," I replied. And I turned to go.

"Wait a minute, Mr. Tashjian."

Oh boy, this is where it gets interesting, I thought to myself. I turned.

"I appreciate the way you came all the way out here by yourself, Mr. Tashjian. Not accompanied by any other federal officers."

Suddenly I was very lonely for some other officers. Thirty, forty, fifty of 'em would have been a big help. Now I'm a man of courage but I'm not a damn fool. Although right about then I wasn't so cocksure about that. The stories about Mr. Capone were enough to bring an atheist to his knees. Even his own men, if he believed they had crossed him, disappeared from the face of the earth. Sometimes showed up at the bottom of the lake, attached to bricks. Big bricks. Rocks of cement. Or they turned up maybe months later in the trunk of a car. Maybe they never showed up at all. Some were known to have met with an accident, a car wreck, a fall from a horse.

"You a gambling man?" Capone asked me then.

"I believe my being here says I'm a gambling man," I replied. I smiled. *May as well go out smiling*, I thought to myself. It's funny, when you're really up against a wall there's this insidious comical character sitting on your shoulder looking for humor in the situation.

"Well, I've got a dog track out there, you might have noticed. The dogs'll be running tonight. You may as well stick around awhile. It's a long drive."

"I never bet on dogs," I said.

"Thought you said you're a gambling man," he said, laughing at me behind his long slow smile.

"I never bet on dogs," I said again. And inside I was saying, *You bet on one helluva dog this time, Armenian.*

"Well," he drawled out slowly. "You may as well make your gasoline money, since you're all the way out here."

It was beginning to sound like he really thought I'd get all the way back. Maybe a good sign. Or maybe a strategic move in a very high-stakes game of chess.

"Here, I'll tell you what," he said. "You bet on the dog I tell you to bet on. Maybe you'll be lucky."

That sly smile said he was not saying everything he was thinking. His eyes didn't leave me. They didn't even blink. Like he was very absorbed reading my eyes; like they were a book.

"Thank you very kindly," I said.

"Bet two."

You know, all these years that number has stuck in my mind. Every time I have ever seen the number two it comes back to me, the whole scene.

He watched me to see what I would do. I watched him back. It was a standoff. I wasn't going to let him stare me down. Finally, he inclined his head and looked at his fingernails again. One hand, then the other. I turned and left. Not another word was spoken.

When I got down the stairs it was as if a red carpet had been spread out there for my exit, except there was no red carpet. It was a carpet of silence and space. It was eerie how nobody was there to show me out or even acknowledge that I had ever been there. Still, there was this feeling that I was being watched.

I walked out. Didn't look back. Walked to my car and sat for a minute, thinking. I thought, *I'll come back for that dog race. Just out of curiosity. See who the people are who gather around this man.*

You see, you couldn't be around Capone without sensing that you were in the presence of a giant. Not just because he was big. He was a mountain of a man, that's certainly true. But not just his body. He had a power about him. A charisma, you might say. In his quiet and gentlemanly way, he was strangely bigger than life. He was intelligent and he was streetwise. He was ruthless and he was kind, gentle in his way. You could be afraid of him and drawn to him at the same time. But one thing you knew—this man would be remembered and talked about for a long time. He was one of a kind, and he would make his mark. He would leave tracks, and people would not forget that he had passed their way. The air was alive with it.

Yeah, I said to myself, *I think I'll stick around.*

So I took off to go get a bite to eat, and then I just cruised around the area getting a feel of the land. *So this is Al Capone's stomping ground,* I thought.

I went back in a couple of hours and nothing was happening. The dog races weren't until pretty late in the evening, it turned out. I had already cased the area, already had a bite to eat, and I didn't feel like I could go into Al's place for a drink, so my options were narrowing down.

I'm a very patient man in certain ways, which contributed, in part, to my strength and perseverance in tracking down these wanted types. But at times I'm very thin on patience. I began to think, *Maybe I'll just go on back to Chicago.*

I headed out of town. But the man and his operation

intrigued me. *No*, I said to myself, *I'm going back*. I turned around. *I'm gonna get a good look while I'm here*, I thought.

When I got back to where the house was—it was a grand house, very large, elegant, with the dog track a few hundred feet away—sure enough, a crowd was gathering. Now, this was something considerably more than I had imagined. People kept coming. And coming and coming. Till there were thousands. People streamed into that place like a river. Not in the house, the house was a sort of private club. There were only forty, fifty, maybe sixty people, at the outside, in the house, where the gambling and drinking was going on. Just how exclusive it was, I don't know. Maybe you had to know Al to get in.

Anyway, this dog-race event going on out in the back was no small operation. I had assumed this was just a hobby sort of thing he had going on. No way. This was big-time gambling. One good thing was that the numbers of people made it easy for me to get lost in the crowd.

I looked at the odds and I thought, *Yeah, I'm gonna make a little bet. I'll just see what this dog number two is gonna do*. So I went up to the window and played the number the big man had given me the tip on. Played to win.

I went out, mingled in the crowd, watched the races, until the race I was interested in came up. Then there he came. My race, my dog. And sure enough, two wins.

Now I had bet only ten dollars. Just enough to satisfy my curiosity. The dog was paying off at thirty-eight dollars and some odd cents for every two dollars. Christ, if I'd been less suspicious, I could easily have made a tidy little bundle for myself. I had two hundred, maybe two hundred fifty dollars on me. I always carried cash. In my line of work you had to be ready for anything.

I kicked myself and went to the window and took a place in the line to collect. Figured it had been an easy hundred ninety or so dollars, which would certainly have taken care of my gasoline, like the man said. Now, bear in mind, a hundred and ninety dollars was a helluva lot more then than it is now.

But before I got up to the window I started thinking, *Hey, I better watch myself pretty carefully out here. There's a damn good chance somebody else is watching me. Yeah, maybe they've got an angle on me. More than maybe.*

So before I got to the front of the line, I ducked out. No way was I gonna get myself in a position where I was obligated to these people in any way. Or where they had anything on me. Even a little ten-dollar bet on a dog.

So I got outta there. While the gettin' was good. I didn't see Al Capone again for four or five months. Then, lucky me, I was given a warrant for his arrest.

I asked around about Capone's whereabouts. I had certain regular informers, but nobody seemed to know of his recent patterns of movement. Like I said before, part of the art of my job of delivering subpoenas and warrants was the element of surprise. If they know you're coming, they disappear.

So I asked around. And got nothing. I went to all the places where I had even half-leads. Maybe he'd be here; maybe he'd be there. No soap. Then I thought, *Suppose I do a flip. Play it the opposite of the rules. Approach Capone with lights flashing and flags waving.*

I went straight to one of his lieutenants. "I'd like to see Mr. Capone," I said. "He knows me."

"What do you wanta see him about?" the guy answered.

"Well," I said, "I've got a warrant for his arrest."

Now, bear in mind, this is not the way the game is

supposed to be played. The one thing you don't do is give the guy you're after warning. But I was playing a hunch. A very long-shot hunch. Setting myself up for an ambush is what I woulda been told, if I had told anybody. But I just did what I did and didn't say boo to anybody I worked with.

Capone's lieutenant smiled. Like he had swallowed a canary. A very slippery canary that went down real smooth. "Well," he said, "Mr. Capone is a pretty nice man. He won't dodge you. You make a date with me when you'll be back, and I'll contact the Boss and see about an appointment. Gimme a coupla days." He held out his hand to shake on it.

I kept my date with the lieutenant. The way I understood it, I was supposed to show up to find out directly from the lieutenant when and where I could talk to the big man. It was a ring toss what kind of reception would be waiting for me.

I chose to go alone. The lieutenant was there, waiting for me. "Okay, Marshal," he said. "You do what I tell you. Go down one block, turn to your left, and look for this address."

He handed me a paper with an address, handwritten. "Big house. Gray brick. Six steps to the door," he said.

I wondered what I was going there for. He didn't say. I didn't ask. Just said, "Thank you very kindly," and shook his hand and walked down the block.

I began to wonder about my smartass plan of playing this one straight. So far, they were being polite to me. But what was I going to meet up with around the corner?

I remembered how cool Mr. Capone had been when I delivered the subpoena. *What is it that makes him so cocksure of himself?* I wondered. The man, it seemed, couldn't be moved. *Maybe that's it,* I thought. *Maybe that's the key to the inside of the man.* I wasn't sure I was very fond of this though.

I rounded the corner on foot. There was the house, gray brick, on the left. The only gray-brick house on the block. It was a lot more than a house, too; it was a goddamn mansion.

There was no address on the building. *Now, that,* I thought, *is interesting.* But there could be no doubt that this was the place that had been described to me.

I went up the steps. Six, just like the man had said. Rang the bell. Waited.

A lady opened the door. Asked me what I wanted.

"I have an appointment," I said. A little vague, but then I wasn't sure why I was there myself. Maybe to see the man himself.

Then again . . . "Who are you?" she asked.

I showed her my credentials. "Tashjian," I said.

"Step right in, Mr. Tashjian," she said.

And who was sitting right there but Mr. Capone himself. "Come to collect on the dog?" he asked, real straight-faced.

I had to give the guy credit. I smiled.

"I hear you got an arrest warrant for me," he said then.

"Yeah, I got an arrest warrant for you." I took a few steps closer to him, held the paper out to him.

"Read it to me," he said. He turned to preening his damn fingernails.

I read, "To any United States marshal or other authorized officer. You are hereby commanded to arrest Alphonse Capone and bring him forthwith before the nearest available United States commissioner to answer to a complaint charging him with violation of federal acts, concerning the sale and distribution of alcohol and alcoholic beverages." It had the date and the name of the United States Commissioner Beitler.

Capone was unmoved. Like I had just read him a definition of the word *table* from the dictionary.

"Now," I said, "what do you want me to do with you, Al?" The familiarity of using his first name surprised myself. When I heard it come out of my own mouth, I wasn't sure how he'd take that.

He looked up. Smiled like the Mona Lisa at me. It was a long time before he spoke. At least it seemed long to me. "What's on the menu?" he finally asked.

"Well now, we government people are always courteous, y' know. You know me, Mr. Capone. I wouldn't want to be rough and tough or anything like that. I'm not anxious to put handcuffs on anybody or use a weapon. Now I know you to be a gentleman . . ."

He smiled. Just with his eyes. Nodded slightly. As if to say, Yes, go on. . . .

"You can come with me now . . ."

He looked through me like I hadn't said anything at all. Well, clearly that option was out.

"Or, we can make arrangements to meet at the Federal Building. Tomorrow."

"Nine o'clock," he said.

"Dearborn Street side," I said. "Not so noticeable." He was there. Accompanied by three other gentlemen. I went up to them.

"We're ready, Marshal," Capone said.

"Who are these gentlemen?" I asked.

"My attorneys," he replied.

Well, okay, I guess he was entitled to his legal representation. But I was beginning to doubt the wisdom of meeting on the Dearborn Street side of the building. The usually deserted side. I had just thought to save the situ-

31

ation from turning into a circus of people gawking and cameras flashing and ugly speculation in the papers. Now, there I was, a hundred thirty pounds soakin' wet, surrounded by four guys as big as horses. Guys not noted for their kindness. And nobody around, thanks to my thinking ahead.

I turned and led the way into the building. We rode up in the elevator without a word. Eighth floor, commissioner's office. At that time the commissioner was Henry C. Beitler.

"Mr. Beitler," I said, "this is Al Capone. And his attorneys."

Beitler asked me to read the warrant to Capone, and this time it included the amount of bond.

Capone and his attorneys were of one accord. Unmoved. Then one of the attorneys spoke. "Your honor, Mr. Commissioner, we have the bond here."

Talk about calm and cool. And so damn polite. Always, at every turn, they were so proper, so respectful. But there was something else in it. You could smell it. No wonder they were always so unruffled by things like warrants for the arrest of the big man. They had their angles all figured out long before anybody ever caught up with them. It was beginning to take the shape of a pattern.

Slippery, I thought. *We'll never get him on anything. Never make it stick. You can see it in their eyes, in the slack muscles of their faces. The subtle arrogance. They're so damn sure they're six jumps ahead of the system. And damned if they aren't. Well, we'll keep trying. And maybe one of these days. . . .*

Beitler was containing his anger. He knew they had it wired. But what could he do? "Okay," he said. "You're released. Your attorney knows when you appear." He spun around and stomped out. The door slammed behind him.

The handwriting was on the wall. We wouldn't get Capone this time. But we'd keep trying.

Sure enough. When the trial came up, Capone beat the rap. He was acquitted. Walked away. Some technicality. The government had been trying to bring him in for a long time. That was the first time they had gotten this far. And I was the guy who brought him in. It was history. Gray-fedora man. I used to think of Capone that way. He was history all right. I knew it. And I was part of it, too. And at least it had gone as far as trial before Capone slithered out of our grasp. Maybe next time we'd get him and keep him.

Now, you have to understand how Capone worked. We didn't have the whole picture then; a lot of it has come to light in the years since. We knew he controlled a lot of politicians, that he had the police force in his pocket, but we didn't know what a far-reaching stranglehold he had on the city of Chicago and environs.

You see, he had the city divided into four sections, north, south, east, and west. Each division had its own lieutenant in charge. These were ruthless men, men Capone could trust no matter what. He had a billion-dollar operation in alcohol and gambling, and these were the guys who ran the show. They were like extensions of Capone, acting for him. The man never did his dirty work himself. Matter of fact, he was so protected behind his lieutenants and his bodyguards and his attorneys, rumor had it he was never even shot at, not once. Not that there weren't people who wanted it done, but nobody was damn fool enough to try. It would have been suicide to go up against Capone.

Now, you understand that his business was in alcohol and gambling. No drugs. Somehow, over time, people have come to think of Al Capone as controlling a big narcotics business, but it wasn't true. He was adamant about that. If one of his people were found messing with drugs, for money or for his own habit, that man was gone.

Now, the policemen knew it would be foolhardy to stop Capone or any of his people on any violation at all. They just let 'em go through no matter what they did. Because not only would they get off, but the policeman would find himself suspended. Or fined. Or even without a job if he had gotten too smart.

You wanta talk about power—Capone's power was entrenched like nobody else has ever been able to match. All the way up, all the way down. From the rookie policemen on up, from the governor on down.

Now, the problems Capone did have came from some of his middlemen. Guys who got too big for their britches and tried to skim off some funds for themselves or share in the power. Take over some of the business themselves. That's where the arguments started. And y' know where they ended. Bottom of the lake.

Now, here's the way it worked. Each lieutenant was responsible for a large territory, and it was up to him to pick the men who would hustle the beer and alcohol in his district. The beer came in fifty-five-gallon barrels. Tap beer. And the alcohol came in five-gallon cans. Beer sold to the illegal distributors for fifty-five dollars a barrel. The price went up and down on the alcohol because they couldn't always get enough to meet the demand. The beer was different. They made it themselves in back rooms and basements. They could make it fast and they did. So with the beer they kept up with the demand, and that kept the price constant.

Now, each lieutenant appointed men in his district to run the beer- and alcohol-hustling business. The names of these men were sent to Capone himself. He had his confidential men check up on 'em, find out if they were reliable. If they had any weak spot that could cause trouble. If anybody had blackmail on them or anything like that that would cause them to be a weak link in the organization. Once in a while they made a mistake. Not too many, but once in a while one of the guys hired to handle the racket would figure he could outsmart the organization. This guy wouldn't last long.

Now, the way they worked was like this. They'd have a truck to haul the barrels of beer and the five-gallon cans of alcohol and deliver it to the speakeasies. We called 'em saloons in the old days. The truck would have lettering on it that was very close to that of a well-known, recognized store or company name, except one or two letters would be different. This was so they could give the impression of a legitimate outfit but not be held for wrongfully using a real company's name. Like if there were a Century Paint Store, they might put Centurion Paints and paint it in the same style as the legitimate company. This enabled them to travel easily and mingle with the other cars and trucks and not stick out. Another thing they did to their trucks sometimes was put a big dark cover over the back, like an awning, maybe dark brown or black. Then they could move through the streets at night like a shadow, unnoticed.

Now, a truck would pull up to the rear of a speakeasy, in the back alley, and dump a couple of barrels of beer, or half a dozen maybe, and some cans of alcohol and disappear. This was without the owner's approval. That's an important point. Y' see, Capone's people were the sole source of the alcohol these saloon keepers needed. That was part of the job of Capone's outfit, to make sure that nobody else elbowed their way into the business. If they tried, they were gone. A memory. So they were the sole source of supply, they made certain of that. And then they also controlled the quantities. That way they could keep the price up by keeping the supply just a little under the demand.

Now, the beer and alcohol was delivered in quantities determined by Capone's lieutenants. And the owner of the saloon was held accountable for it, whether he liked it or not. A collector would show up in the next few days, and the owner had better cough up the money. The collector would be one of the lieutenant's men.

"We left you three barrels of beer, at fifty-five dollars a barrel; that's a hundred sixty-five dollars you owe. And we gave you two cans of alcohol . . ." at whatever the price was at that time. And the owner had to pay, whether he'd ordered the stuff or not.

Now, this was hundred-proof alcohol, not whiskey. The saloon keepers used it to make their own whiskey. They had their own coloring and other ingredients. In fact, the other ingredients were also controlled by Capone's outfit but through different channels.

Now, this system worked pretty well most of the time; Capone had a stranglehold on the business. But there was one small snag in the system at the delivery point. Every now and then when they would dump the beer and alcohol in the back alley behind a speakeasy, one of these fellas under the lieutenant would bring in an extra five-gallon can of alcohol. Now, he was counting on that part of human nature that wants to get away with something. Especially off of somebody who has got him by the neck.

According to the system, the collector would come by a few days later to get the money for the number of barrels and cans that were supposed to have been delivered. The saloon owner would know that he had gotten one more can of alcohol than he was being charged for. Now, any guy tryin' to make a killing off the illegal sale of alcohol is not apt to be a guy who is going to speak up to his jailers and say, "Thank you, kind sir, but I believe I owe you for one more," right? At least that's what these smart guys were counting on.

Then, in a day or two, the guy setting himself up to skim a little off the organization's business would show up and say, "Sorry, we made an error. We need to collect for one more gallon of alcohol." And he would pocket the price. And he would get away with it. For a while. Maybe.

But then one day some dim-witted saloon keeper would say to the collector, "What? Three cans? I thought I got four this week. . . ." Or the owner would have the money all ready for the collector, and the amount would be too much.

"Whaddaya mean, you're payin' me for what was delivered?" the collector would ask. "I only delivered so many cans, so many barrels. How the hell did this other alcohol business get in here? We don't know nothin' about this."

"Maybe the office made a mistake," the owner would say. He wouldn't wanta get mixed up in anything.

The collector would figure out right away what was going on. "Yeah," he'd say, smiling. "Probably the office made a mistake. Awful lot of speakeasys, and an awful lot of beer and alcohol to keep track of. Thanks." And he'd take the money and turn it in and report to the lieutenant what had transpired.

"That's okay, we'll take care of it," the lieutenant would say. And they'd watch the delivery guy like a hawk. Probably just some poor workin' man tryin' to hustle a little on the side and make a buck for himself off of Prohibition. Maybe he had a family to feed, y' know.

But now Capone's men had their eye on him. One false move, and it was all over. He was gone. He just wouldn't show up again. Now you see him, now you don't.

It just wasn't smart to try to outsmart Capone and his lieutenants. Like an ant trying to walk across the street in front of a bulldozer. It just wasn't worth trying.

These men working for the lieutenant were dangerous men, I'm tellin' ya. They were no sissies. They were tough guys. They had to be tough. They had to protect the truck; they had to protect the whole barrel-dumping procedure; they had to deal with the owners and either collect the money or do things to make them pay up if they backed off. It could get messy. There was no tiptoeing through the tulips for them.

Now remember, Capone controlled the entire city of Chicago. Once he had the control of the governor and the police departments and the captains of every precinct, he had no trouble delivering the illegal alcohol or running illegal gambling joints all over the city. Or enforcing his own terms, doing business however he chose to do business. There was simply no one who could stop him.

Capone had a Las Vegas–type gambling operation long before Las Vegas developed. It was all illegal, of course, but I think that's part of what turned him on. He was a man who got a kick out of beating the establishment.

He'd started in the rackets when he was just a young man. Worked for John Torrio in New York City. Now it was also through John Torrio that the young Capone got started in Chicago. Torrio wanted a piece of the action in Chicago. Greedy, y' know. New York wasn't big enough. Well, actually New York was divided up among the various power lords, and you couldn't really expand there. So Torrio decided to branch out to the city of Chicago, which was wide open then. Raw territory. Almost.

At that time Jimmy Colisimo was the chief power in Chicago. But he was small peanuts. Didn't even aspire to more than just his small-time prostitution business, fronted by a well-known fancy restaurant. He had the "in" place, y' know, fancy entertainment and all. The prima-donna entertainers of the day. All the important people went to his restaurant; it was a real showplace. Nice place. And he made a damn good profit from the operation.

Now, Torrio saw the city of Chicago as a ripe berry just waiting to be picked. By somebody just like him, with a flair for organization. Torrio looked, he saw, and he said, "Let's move in there."

So he approached Colisimo and said, "Look, this is an open town. There's enough room for both of us. Let's get into the gambling and beer business; that's where the money is. We'll work together."

"Not interested," Colisimo replied.

"Look. I've got a man I can send in here to handle the beer and alcohol business," Torrio said. "No sweat to you. We'll just start with your existing organization and expand from there. I'm gonna bring my man out here and introduce you to him, and then we'll talk some more."

"Not interested," Colisimo said.

But Torrio went ahead anyway. And he brought in his flunky, young Al Capone. And the legend began.

Capone, at that time, was just a young hoodlum. He did what he was told by John Torrio. He was tough, y' understand, but a nobody. But Torrio had confidence in him. So he brought young Al Capone into Chicago to work for Jimmy Colisimo, whether Colisimo liked it or not. And the job Torrio gave Capone was to hustle the customers in and out of the prostitution operation.

Now, Capone's job was to stand on the steps or up on the balcony—it was a three-story building, and it had a big curved stairway going around—and say, "C'mon, keep movin'." They wanted the business to be brisk, y' see, at two dollars a flop. That's all it was, two dollars.

"C'mon, keep movin', keep movin'." That was it. That was Al Capone's start in the city of Chicago. Well, he also acted as a sort of bouncer if there was any trouble, y' know. But basically his job was just to hustle 'em in and out.

At the time Capone came in, I was just a civilian, a regular citizen. I had nothing to do with the law at that time; I was just a kid on the street.

So John Torrio went back to New York, tended to his business, whatever. And then pretty soon he came back to Chicago and he made another proposal to Colisimo.

"Hey look," he said, "this is a wide-open town. A virgin town. We can hustle beer in here and make ourselves a lot of money."

Colisimo still wasn't interested.

So Torrio called a meeting with the three of them—Colisimo, himself, and Al Capone. Now he had the edge, of course, because it was two to one. "Look, Colisimo," he said, "whether you like it or not, Al is gonna hustle Chicago on this beer business. He's gonna be the boss of it, whether you like it or not."

And what did Colisimo do? He still refused to go along with it. He wasn't used to associating with big-time gangsters, and he really wasn't interested in doing so. He just wanted to run his small-time operation, make his nice little profit, and keep these guys out of his hair.

Colisimo didn't want to get in over his head flaunting any big-scale violation of federal laws, the beer and booze laws. Now, he was selling booze in his own place, y' understand; but it was quiet, it was small time, and he had the local power to keep them from closing in on him. He had a very tidy little operation, in fact. Made a nice profit, was treated like somebody, and exercised all the power he needed.

He controlled the first ward, y' see, and that was all

he needed to protect his own operation. There were fifty wards in the city, and the first ward was a very prestigious ward. Controlled maybe two hundred thousand votes in the ward. Colisimo ran a high-class restaurant, attracted high-class clientele, employed the big-name entertainers of the day; he was somebody. Jimmy Colisimo. Hobnobbed with class. Why fix the roof if it ain't leakin'?

But John Torrio saw Colisimo as either a help or a hindrance to his own plans. And Colisimo refused to be a help. Now, Colisimo used to like to ride the horses in Lincoln Park. It was a public park with a stretch of horse trails and picnic grounds. Very pretty and well kept up and a nice peaceful place to go and relax. Colisimo had his own saddle horses, used to go riding with his mistress. She was an actress.

Colisimo had been riding horses for years; he was an excellent rider. And one day when he just happened to be riding along, he had a riding accident. Found him dead on the horse trail in the park. A head injury, looked like a riding accident. Maybe the horse had thrown him, nobody knew; nobody ever saw anything or proved anything. But one thing was clear. Jimmy Colisimo was definitely out of business. Enough about saying no to John Torrio when he made a friendly offer to go into business together.

Now, Capone started gaining momentum. Started slow and easy, but he was building. He made it his business to meet with the politicians. He got to know the aldermen (the equivalent of city councilmen) and the ward committeemen of both parties, Republican and Democrat. Then he arranged to meet the higher-ups—the governor, people like that.

When Len Small ran for governor, Capone donated a lot of money, enough to make sure Len Small would win. Then he supported the state attorney general too, Carlstrom at the time. And he gave money to the committee-men to help elect the candidates they controlled. And to certain judges, so they would be reelected.

It didn't take long before Capone had all these people in the palm of his hand. Before they knew it, he had power over all the people with power. If he had bought one or two, or three or four—which is what they thought he was doing—sure, they'd owe him some favors, but that was all. But it seemed like they slept through it or chose not to see, because suddenly Al Capone had tied up the power structure of the entire city of Chicago. Law makers, law enforcers, power wielders at every level. That's how he did it. Step-by-step, he just arranged to meet people; he was friendly, supportive of whatever suited him. He made donations, payoffs, and then he had them all in his pocket. The whole bunch of 'em. Easy as pie.

Pretty soon the judges in the city of Chicago became know as the Cash Register Judges. They had a price for everything. Al Capone's people could get anything they wanted—for a price. Just pay off the judge or the judge's people. Get somebody out of a violation, a ticket, a jail sentence, an arrest, anything. Cash Register Judges.

Everybody knew it, and nobody would mess with it. Some young upstart lawyer or police sergeant with an attack of conscience would rise up with his hat full of nobility and try to perform his rightful duty, and he'd be out of a job. That's all there was to it.

Capone was not a stupid man. He built his empire of power very carefully, one brick at a time. From the bottom up. He counted on one thing. That he could find enough men with a price tag on their conscience to fill all the positions of power with them. And he would own them. He was right. There were enough men in public service who were willing to sell out so that somebody like Capone

42

could buy a whole city and run it like a puppeteer. Probably still could today.

But one thing limited him. Capone could never make any inroads with the federal people. Not one inch. And eventually that was his downfall. He was indicted, found guilty of income-tax evasion, and sent to Alcatraz to serve his time. After serving time and being released, he went to Florida, where he died.

Now, Capone had an interesting strategy. He disarmed the people by playing a sort of Robin Hood. Exactly who he was robbing nobody knew, but it must have been the rich because there was no doubt he was cleaning up somewhere. Big-league takes. But he distributed a lot of it to the poor. Taking money from the rich and giving it to the poor, now that gave him a hell of an image.

There were a lot of poor in those days. It wasn't as simple as living in the lap of plenty like it is for most people today. People had to struggle to find a job, make a buck, feed a family. And this is something people don't seem to know or don't seem to remember about Al Capone. Maybe it's a case of selective memory, I don't know. He did some pretty heavy operations, big-time gangster stuff, all that, so they want to make him out to have been all bad. But nobody's all bad. And Al Capone did some things that really helped people. Listen to this—and every word I'm telling you is true, I swear it.

Al Capone set up more bread lines and shelters to take care of people; gave out more jobs, more food, more money; arranged for medical care; distributed Christmas baskets—everything you can think of that people need when their luck ran low—I'm tellin' ya, he did more to help the common people than all the government agencies and charity places put together. You can bet he endeared himself to the public that way, and how. And so he became sort of untouchable, y' know what I mean? He was a local hero, at least in the beginning. The people had the hard evidence—they had food in their bellies, a couple of bucks in their pockets, jobs, even if they were flunky jobs—and whatever they had was only because Al Capone's men were busy arranging all this. And they made sure the people knew who it came from too.

This man, Capone, cared about the people's problems when nobody else seemed to; that was the way the people saw it. So it appeared he was a good man to have involved in the local government. Now, maybe he had his own personal motives for doing what he did, I grant you that, but nevertheless he did a lot of good for the people.

Now, like I said, a lot of people don't know these things about Al Capone. He's been portrayed as a hard and bloody hoodlum. The legend has grown over the years until he's remembered as something he wasn't. He wasn't all bad. He wasn't a crazed killer. The man was sensitive to the pulse of the people. He was a gentleman, a soft-spoken man, and he had his eye on the needs of the average man. That was the image he had; that was the image he wanted to have. And he was enough of a strategist to put together an organization to carry off that image. If he wanted the people to believe he was a good man, then he had to do some good things to convince them. And he did. He did a lot of good.

But these things don't come cheap, y' know. Public works, welfare operations. You multiply these efforts by a whole lot of people and you've got a pretty hefty tab. Now, Capone was getting his money somewhere; it sure wasn't coming out of his own pocket and the goodness of his heart. He had gambling operations. And it's interesting,

I think, that with all the money he had rolling in he had the foresight and the shrewdness to invest it in his image and in his long-range political plans.

Now, here's a thought. Why do all these politicians, and they still do it today, why do they spend ten times more on their campaign to get into office than they will ever earn once they get the job? Because they're sacrificing themselves, dedicating their career to public service. Don't kid yourself. There's more in it than money. And these people are not Florence Nightingale or Albert Schweitzer.

Now, I've observed all this right up close, having been involved with a lot of politicians in the city of Chicago back in the early days. And two things are very clear. One, they always get in touch with some mysterious flow of money coming from somewhere that far exceeds the publicly known salary for their job. And two, these people are a peculiar breed. They need power. It's like they feed on power the way a vampire feeds on blood.

Now, Al Capone understood all this. He knew the minds of these public figures, and he knew how to get them in the palm of his hand. The man was a natural psychologist. First thing Al Capone did was donate a lot of money to both sides, so he was guaranteed to come out a winner. Remember, the man understood gambling. He knew how to play the game and always came out ahead.

He started with the local politicians, and he spread out from there. Spread outward, spread upward, building his sphere of influence quietly, steadily. Nobody seemed to know that he was buying everybody else. It's like a snowball on a hill. You take snow and roll it into a snowball and keep pushing, and it gets bigger and bigger. But it's silent, you see. If they're not watching you, nobody knows what you're doing. And you start rolling the snowball down the hill, and it gains momentum and keeps getting bigger and

45

bigger, and pretty soon it gets so big that you'd better get out of the way or it'll kill ya—that was Capone with his political machine. He was a powerhouse. He just sneaked up on everybody and quietly got the people in power eating out of his hand, and suddenly he was running the city of Chicago. And nobody was in a position to stand up to him. It would have been suicide. Politically and, well, sometimes worse. Take my word for it; I was there.

The loyalty he inspired was something else. Well, I say inspired, but the inspiration was in an unsavory form. It was well known that anyone who turned on Capone disappeared; it was as simple as that. Went for a swim, they called it. To the bottom of the lake. And when it was over—any of the incidents connected to his organization — suddenly nobody knew anybody. The people who had been seen together a week before, a month before, nobody knew each other anymore; that's how close-mouthed they were. They just closed up ranks, and it was as if nothing had ever happened. He was a master all right, and his organization was tight.

I remember one time when two of Capone's top men disappeared. The one fella was cross-eyed. The other one was a tough you wouldn't want to tangle with. Capone had a rule and all his people knew it. He promised that "everybody would be paid properly." And he always kept his promise. Now you can interpret that in more ways than one. These two guys were never found. Or at least they were never identified. If they were found, their bodies were beyond recognition. To my knowledge, this particular case has never been solved in all these years. Nobody knew what went wrong, what these two men did, or what happened to them. At least nobody would talk. The men just went bye-bye, as they used to say.

Capone was the law in those days. And he treated

everybody equal. Did what he said was to be done, you were well taken care of. Did otherwise, you were gone.

Now, Capone had women. He liked the good life. Fine clothes, find food, glamorous women. He could have any woman he wanted. Always had a woman on his arm. Beauties. Made Hollywood women look anemic. He'd throw big parties, have a lot of highfalutin' people there. Big names. Politicians, actresses, money people. The women in those days didn't wear a lot of makeup like they do now, just a little, but they looked prettier, I think with just their natural beauty. And the men were men. No hair spray or earrings like these people today.

Those parties were all right. There was Prohibition, and we got a certain joy out of breaking the rules, y' know. The booze flowed and the music played and the people would party all night long. Dance till it rained. It was an era.

Now, as I said earlier, these lieutenants would never mention any names on the telephone. For instance, if I was one of Capone's lieutenants, maybe my code was five-for-six, and if I wanted to say Al Capone's number, say three-for-four, I would telephone and then whoever answered I would say, "This is five-for-six. I want to speak to three-for-four."

Five-for-six by that time had been checked out and they knew you were okay; then you went on with your conversation. This was in case of wiretapping by the government; they wouldn't be able to prove who five-for-six or three-for-four were. There were no names, only numbers that could be anybody anywhere, so they were protected. It was different in speakeasies where they used the telephone; being a public phone it didn't incriminate the owners.

Drugs in
Al Capone's Chicago

DURING THE AL CAPONE days in Chicago, drugs and narcotics hardly existed. Now, drugs were around, y' understand. But Al Capone was adamantly against drugs, and I mean adamantly. He would have no part of them. And he made sure that none of the men in his organization had any part of them. And since Al Capone ruled the city of Chicago and his men had their hands on most of the substantial flow of money in the town, Al Capone's personal opinion tended to curb drug traffic throughout the entire city.

If one of Al Capone's people were found to have anything to do with drugs, either using them himself or selling or dealing in any way, he was given the axe. Now, I don't mean they would give him the car-trunk treatment, but that man would be gone. Like a leaf blowin' in the wind. Gone. Gone from the organization and gone from town. And nobody would know where.

Al Capone was no dummy, y' know. He was a very intelligent man. And it's my guess he didn't want to take a chance that any of his men would get themselves in a position where their alertness would be compromised. He wanted his men clearheaded. Now, that's just my guess. For all I know he may have had some bad experience himself with drugs back in his New York days; I don't know. But it's my guess that it was a matter of control over his men. That's the kind of man he was.

In those days in Chicago there would be maybe thirty narcotics cases in a whole month. Compare that to the number of cases today; it was hardly a drop in the ocean. You didn't see drugs and users and pushers on every street corner like you do today. The few rare cases that occurred were handled through the United States marshal's office, so I was aware of them. Cocaine, morphine.

The cases were reviewed then by the commissioner, who was an attorney. Now, this man would review each case one by one, analyze the person and the situation, and decide what was best to do. He would decide if it was worthwhile to take the case to a federal court. Take up a federal judge's time and the public money and all. If it involved a big dealer, then maybe he'd pursue it. But if it was just some poor bloke hooked on the stuff, the commissioner would recommend a treatment program. The attitude then was to try to help the addict. Try to help him get off the stuff. Generally the commissioner would just lay a fine on the person and give him thirty or sixty days, maybe a little longer.

Now, the commissioner would work together with a doctor. This was a federal doctor, a doctor on the rolls in the government service. He was on duty in the Federal Building. Same building we were in.

The doctor would look the addict over, run some tests, and determine what he was usin'. If he was shootin' or sniffin' or smokin' or what, and how much, how often. He could tell in a half hour of talking with a man how long he'd been taking drugs.

Then the commissioner would evaluate the case. If he determined to just give the guy a fine and a stint in the county jail, the case would be assigned to the county and the addict would be sent to the jail in his area.

Now, before he left the Federal Building, the doctor

would give him a shot of whatever it was he was on. To make him feel good, y' know, so he wouldn't go through withdrawal suddenly. That can be deadly. Then during his sixty days in jail, or however many days he got, maybe a hundred and twenty, they'd give him more, but continually less and less of the drug. Wean him off it, slowly, until his body had adjusted to using only a little and finally none at all. They'd keep a close eye on him, and very carefully control his drug intake. They knew what they were doin'. And if a guy had half a brain, he'd appreciate the treatment, and he'd stay off the stuff. Clean up his life while he had a chance. But most of 'em didn't.

We had a saying. Once a user, always a user. We saw it happen too many times; they'd get cured and they'd go back on it. But I have to admit, once in a while the program really worked.

This one jail that I knew about—we took several cases out there—had Red Grange's father as the sheriff. I'm talkin' about Red Grange the famous football player, seventy-seven was his number. Now, Red Grange's father got some of these drug cases. And he'd give 'em a little shot, and then cut it down, cut it down. Get 'em off the stuff and send 'em on their way. With some strong admonitions. And maybe some of those boys would come back and maybe they wouldn't. And if one came back, damned if the doctors wouldn't be patient with him and put him through the program again. Try to ease him down.

But we used to say, "Once a user, always a user." They oughta tell 'em that. Not when they're in jail, but when they're still kids in school. Let 'em know. Scare the bejabers outa the kids so they'll never get started. It's a crime to be lax on the subject. These kids are killin' themselves. The dealers are killin' 'em. Just to make some money for themselves, y' know. Now, that is a crime.

50

Now, there was this one case that I will never forget. I came into the office tired as hell this one day. Been out on a case for days. I was trudgin' over to my desk and before I could sit down I saw these two ladies sittin' there. An older one and a younger one. Later I found out they were mother and daughter.

Now, what I saw was enough to startle me outa my weary state. Here were these ladies' bosoms stickin' out in front of me. Hangin' out right over their brassieres. And they were pulsing. It was funny in a way, but on closer look it was scary. It was so unnatural. I didn't know what was wrong with 'em. There was this fuzz on their bosoms, coming right out of their nipples. I said, "Hey, Captain Carr! What the hell is goin' on here? I'm tired. I worked all night. I don't need any more trouble."

Now, a man shoots the stuff into his arms to get it into his bloodstream so he can get quicker action. What I didn't know was that a woman, once she has shot her arms full of holes, will shoot it directly into her nipples. This is supposed to get it into her system faster, and that's important to a heavy user. Makes the drug work faster.

So I talked to these two ladies to get some dope. I mean information, not dope. They looked to me like they were some woman and girl from skid row. They were dressed like a coupla bums, all disheveled. Probably hadn't changed clothes in days. Or had a bath. Now, a doper will sell anything to get money for drugs. It turned out they had sold their good clothes. Furs and everything.

The husband-father was a very well-known man, one of the outstanding physicians in the world. I forget now just what his work was, but he had made a name for himself in certain circles. And they lived well; you bet they did.

But here were his wife and daughter, sunk to a level that is hard to describe. A human tragedy. They had every opportunity to live a nice life, and here they were all messed up, hooked on drugs. They must've started out small, just takin' a little. For kicks, y' know. And takin' it and takin' it, until they got to a state where they craved it and couldn't go without.

Dope dealers will give it to you free to get you started, y' know. But in those days it cost like hell; it wasn't cheap on the streets like now. Those dealers were greedy. They'd rather sell to the rich who could pay a good price. At least, at first they could.

Well, things got so bad that these two, the mother and daughter, left home. They sank so low they were picked up on the street by the cops. Now, I'm tellin' ya, these were two beautiful women. Under all the misery and the drugs and the self-abuse. Beautiful, both of 'em. Later, when they were all cleaned up, the change was amazing.

The girl was maybe seventeen, eighteen. And the mother looked good. Not when I first saw the two of 'em. Then they looked like something out of a horror movie. But later. Later they looked pretty damn elegant.

So I talked to 'em, and I really wanted to help these two. It makes me sad to see people fall so low because of drugs. I felt sorry for 'em. They couldn't go home. And they couldn't get off the stuff without help. So I said, "Look, we're gonna help you."

I talked to the captain and told him the things I had learned from talking with the women, and I said, "Let's not make it worse for these people. Let's just see if we can help 'em get their lives straightened out."

And he agreed. These two were not just bums on the street. Nor were they tryin' to make money off other people's misery, like the dealers. Now, those are the ones I'd like to see dealt with severely.

Anyway, we kept these two in our own cell up there

on the eighth floor of the Federal Building for a while and called in the doctor. He got 'em started on a program to ease 'em off the stuff. We brought in some clean clothes; let 'em clean up. Let 'em think about dignity again.

And, y' know, they were so appreciative. You wouldn't believe the difference in their appearance when they weren't controlled by the drugs and they'd cleaned themselves up. And they began to look at life differently, too. They were two very nice people. Elegant people. Good background and all.

'Course for all I know they went back to it. Back on the stuff. "Once a user, always a user," that's what we used to say. But maybe sometimes a person is strong enough to stay clean. I hope those two made it.

A Bullet from Mangano

DAGO LAWRENCE MANGANO. EVERYBODY knew his name. A classy guy. Small-time businessman turned big-time Prohibition operator. There was a warrant out for him and it was mine.

Mangano was one of Capone's men. In charge of operations over a section of the west side of Chicago. I took the case myself. I didn't have any regular partner and didn't think I needed one. I was young, brash. Immortal, y' know.

So I went out on it alone. Started working slowly, trying to get an earful here and there, find out what I could. I had my ways, y' know. I've never told anybody in all these years what the ways of the government men are. It could hurt somebody, even today.

Well, one way or another, I vowed, I'd find Mangano. Where his office was, where he lived, or where he hung out. I had my informers and usually they were reliable. A little slow, maybe inaccurate sometimes, but eventually they would come through. Trouble was, I didn't always have the time or the patience to wait for them to come through.

So this time I went to a barbershop in the general vicinity of where I'd heard Mangano had been seen. The barbershop was on Harrison and Halstead streets, the southeast corner. It's probably still there. Well, maybe.

I strolled in there real casual, like I lived around there, and asked for a haircut. And I listened. After a while I

54

heard "The Dago" come up in conversation. Ah, I was on his trail; I could smell it. Now, they could have been talking about somebody else, but my antenna told me they were talking about my man. It slipped by in the conversation pretty fast and I didn't get enough information to give me what I needed to make my move, but I knew I was getting close. This was his territory. People knew him.

Now, you can't get a haircut every day in the same place. I waited a few days and went back for a shave. And listened. Nobody mentioned my man. Finally I did. "I'm supposed to meet somebody here," I said.

"Who ya meeting?" the barber asked.

"Well, I don't know about sayin' who. But I'm supposed to meet him here about now. And I don't see him. Now, I've gotten my shave and I can't use another haircut so soon. And I haven't got time to wait all day."

I was hoping, of course, that this curious conversation would turn up some other information I could use. It aroused the barber's interest all right. "Who is it you're waiting for?" he asked.

"Just a guy. A guy that comes around here," I replied.

"To my shop?" he wanted to know.

"Naw. Not *in* the shop," I said. "I'm just supposed to see him walk by here and then go meet him. Y' know how it is."

A look on his face told me he knew what kind of business I was talking about. Or what kind of business I wanted him to think I was talking about.

"Oh," he said, "I know. One of the Dago's people?"

Sly, I thought, nodding.

"Why don'tcha just go over to his place?" the barber asked then.

I thought a minute. Now, I didn't want him to think

I didn't know where the Dago's place was. "I don't know . . ." I said, hesitatingly.

"Sure," he said, "just go on over there. Maybe his man got tied up or somethin'."

Now, that struck me as funny. *Maybe his man got tied up or somethin'.* Here I was about to tie up Mangano himself.

The barber had nodded toward the street, up a ways. I didn't know exactly where "over there" was supposed to mean, but I figured I was getting closer.

"Well, maybe I will," I said. "It changes our arrangement though."

"So! The guy's late. You got business?"

"Yeah," I said.

And when I left I headed in the direction he had indicated. I looked around. The dominant building was a sort of triangular shape. Different. I figured I'd just hang around there and see if anything noticeable was going on.

What I had was a warrant for the arrest of Dago Lawrence Mangano himself. "Violation of the Prohibition Act" was how it read. These guys were into a lot more than just selling booze, of course, but that was how the warrant read in legal terms.

I wandered around that locale, sniffing. Looked over the cars parked there, figuring it might come in handy to recognize a certain car later. There were cars, all right. An unusual number of fancy ones, Cadillacs and the like. Big cars. Expensive ones. I had no use for taking the license numbers at that time; they didn't mean anything to me. But I'd gotten an impression that could be important. This just might be the clue I was looking for to help me smoke out Mangano.

Later I sent one of my informers over there to see what he could find out. One guy hanging around the neighborhood asking too many questions isn't good. My informer came back with the information I wanted. Dago Lawrence Mangano's office was in that triangular building. That was where his people reported to him.

So I watched. I had a description of Mangano, but I had never seen him in person up to that point. I hung out there for a few days. Wanted to be comfortable in the neighborhood. No matter how casual you try to be, it shows if you're not comfortable. You look like a foreigner in the neighborhood, and people sense that. They can smell the strangeness between you and the place.

The first day that I saw Mangano himself I didn't make a move on him. I wanted to watch his schedule and make note of his moves before I went in. Then a few days later I saw him come out of the building and get in his car. Alone.

I followed him from a distance. There he was in the palm of my hand, but I wasn't ready to go in after him. It was important to me to see where he was going, who he was tied up with. Information like that, identifying a whole chunk of Capone's network, could be a lot more valuable than bringing in just one man.

I followed him. Wherever he was going, he took a strange circuitous route. Maybe he knew he was being followed. He zigzagged around town and finally eluded me. Now, I figured he was on guard. He knew somebody was after him. I would have to be more careful than ever. So I stayed away. Watched cautiously, from a distance. I knew my moment would come again; it was just a matter of time.

Then, suddenly, it was there. A gift, sooner than I had expected it. I had gotten some information from one of my informers about a certain building that Mangano frequented. Not only Mangano but some of his pals as well. I didn't know what was going on there, but I did know that my chances of finding an opportunity to apprehend Mangano had just doubled.

So this time I took my time. Waited for just the right moment. I got to know the neighborhood pretty well, both Mangano's office building and the other place where he went regularly. The comings and goings of Mangano and his people were surprisingly open. I was able to identify a number of his companions by then.

Now, you have to understand, a government man, a United States deputy marshal about to deliver a federal warrant, couldn't just go up to somebody and show them *reason* for bringing them in. It wasn't safe to approach these people, especially when you had news for them that they didn't want to hear. You had to be very careful. You could get yourself shot at real easily.

You're liable to get killed any minute in this business, that's no exaggeration. The danger and the challenge were a lot of what I wanted; they were why I had been anxious to get into this business in the first place. Examining papers for the Internal Revenue Service, working in an office, that was never my cup o' tea. I wanted excitement.

But even when you're a guy who wants excitement, it doesn't mean you want to die for it. You gotta be careful. Too many guys get shot and are never heard from again. Y' see, if you have a search warrant it's difficult enough, but I didn't even have a search warrant to get me in places. What I had were warrants for arrest. These people do not generally take kindly to those.

The stickiest part is that you'll find yourself in big trouble if you bring in someone other than the guy you're really after. Brother, you can get in deeper than you can imagine for pulling that. So you have to verify that the person really is the guy you want, not just that you *think* it's the right guy. Or that you own observations *seem* to verify his identity, in your opinion. That's not good enough. It's a tricky business all right. You have to know what you're doing.

Now, I had Dago Lawrence Mangano's description. He was a nice lookin' gentleman. Stocky build, black hair. Stood about five-foot seven. And by this time I had seen him and followed him. But even when you know who your man is, you can't just go up to him and arrest him. There's no way you can know for sure, see. And if he denies he's who you think he is, where do you go from there? Now, he's seen you, and he knows you're after him. No, you've got to be more careful than that. You've got to be sure, sly so, that when you decide to make your move it's a sure thing. You may only have one chance.

You're all alone in a gangster district. This is the mob, the syndicate. And they might not like what you're doing there. An acquaintance of mine, a narcotics agent, had gotten himself killed. So I thought twice before I made my move.

Gangsters think nothing of government men; they'll kill 'em just as they'd shoot a bunch of nuisance snakes. That's all you are to them. Unless . . . you can sneak up on them in such a way as to get them to acknowledge their identity first; then you can present your credentials and announce your purpose before they can get away. And all this in an open situation, like in public or before a number of other people. That way they can't really get away with shooting you. They know you carry a gun too and are trained to use it. If they try anything and you're a jump ahead of them, then they are in big trouble for messing with a government man. It's a tricky business all right.

Well, I parked a few blocks away from the building where Mangano's office was. I had discovered that he took different routes coming and going. He seemed to make a point of not taking the same route two days in a row. Went the same places pretty much, but arrived and left from different directions. I guess when you're breaking the federal law you're entitled to a little paranoia and a few quirky ways. Anyway, I was on to him, and his way of being sneaky wasn't really very imaginative.

So on this particular day I was four blocks away, hoping that Mangano would arrive at his office from a certain direction. Otherwise I might not know if he was there or not. Well, by damn, he came right by me. I saw his car turn the corner in my rearview mirror. And when it passed me, sure enough, there he was. He pulled into the parking lot. I figured to apprehend him in public, out on the sidewalk, as he went to enter the building.

I watched him get out of his car. I approached. I had it in mind to get close enough to him to call out his name. Get him to turn around in response to it. That was all the acknowledgment I needed. I was gonna shout, "Hey! Lawrence Mangano?" He would turn and then I would say, "I'm a government man." And I would serve the warrant. It was gonna be easy. I had rehearsed it. It fit the situation perfectly. I had watched long enough to be sure.

I waited too long. Got too close before calling out to him. Somebody from his organization must have been casing me, who knows for how long. At the very least, I was being watched from a window somewhere as Mangano approached the building. 'Cause just as I was gettin' closer and closer, just as I was about to meet him face to face and speak out, suddenly he took off like a jackrabbit, ran into the building, and—*Crack crack!* Gunshots!

I didn't know where the shots came from or who they were aimed at. And then I felt it. A hit in the right leg. Me! They were for me! And they'd got me, too. It had to have been from the building. They must have seen me comin'. They must have signaled to Mangano somehow from the building. I hadn't seen that. Maybe the whole thing had been a setup. Maybe they had noticed me prowling around the neighborhood asking questions and the like. Maybe it had been the barber on the corner who had tipped 'em off that I was asking around where I shouldn't be. I don't know. What I do know is I still have a scar on my leg to show for it. Right leg, just above the ankle.

So I had been shot, okay. I ran to my car and jumped in and took off. Y' know, when your life is in danger you can run on an injured leg. Just like it was a good leg. Drove right to the hospital. Safe enough place in case they were following. Besides, I didn't know how serious the wound was, and maybe it needed some attention. The doctors kept me there all night.

That night in the hospital this little old lady came to see me. She was a stranger to me; never saw her before in my life. Made me nervous not knowing who in the devil she was. She could have been one of Mangano's people. Watching me. More of that later.

Meanwhile, government officials called Babe. They told her I had been shot. They went over to the house. What they found there was a shock. These guys had met my wife; they knew what a pretty young thing she was. But the person who opened the door had white hair. Just about like it is now, and now she's been nearly eighty-five years on this planet. I'm not exaggerating. From the careless way they had told her on the phone about my being shot, Babe thought I had been killed. She was pregnant at the time, too. And they didn't think to tell her carefully or to explain that it was just a minor wound in the leg.

My poor, dear, sweet wife. She thought I was dead. But at least she didn't lose the baby. The time she lost the baby I was on a different case. This baby turned out to be our second daughter, Marilyn. The first baby, the one that died, was a boy, a big healthy baby nearly eleven pounds. Then came the girls, thirteen and a half months apart. So this Mangano incident was in the year Marilyn was born.

After the gunshot wound, I waited awhile, let the situation cool down. I went to the office, talked to my boss, Capt. Hal Carr. Somebody had to be in charge of the office. There were not more than twenty of us in room 804, deputy marshal's office—and we were taking care of the whole city of Chicago. And out of the country, too. You're talking about eighteen, twenty law enforcement people maybe. When today one police district alone may have two hundred.

So I told Hal what I was doin'. He said, "That's all right. Take your time; be very careful. I know you'll bring him in. You'll get him."

"I got a reputation to keep, Captain," I replied.

He patted me on the back. He was quite a back slapper that Hal Carr. "I know," he said. "Young Hawk. Always gets his man." And he was right.

So I got busy cooking up another way to get to Mangano. Finally I thought, *I've got it. I'll get right inside there.*

I decided that a big cigar would be my ticket. I figured it this way. As long as the head gamblers and Al Capone's top men were smokin' big cigars, I'd start smokin' 'em, too. And this time when I went lookin' for Mangano, I'd just stroll into the building he was in and start puffin' on a big cigar. And what with me bein' five feet four and a half and weighin' a hundred thirty pounds, what with me presentin' a mean picture like that, they'd never give it a thought that I might be a government man. And the funny part of it was I got to liking those damn things, smokin' those big cigars, and to this day they're my second-best love. Of course, I had to take a chance that none of Mangano's men had seen me up close enough to recognize me. I figured this new cigar-smokin' image might throw 'em off. Anyway, it was worth a try.

So I was hangin' around in the hallway, smokin' a big cigar and chewin' the fat with the guys that hung out there. And there was Mangano coming down the staircase. "Hey, Pops! How are ya?" I called out.

He looked at me like he didn't know me. Or like he couldn't remember where he had seen me or what. He turned to a guy he knew. "Who the hell is this?" he asked.

"Oh, you know me." I lifted my lapel, showing the shield of the United States deputy marshal's office, and flashed him my credentials. Real quick, in front of witnesses, in a public place. That's the best way, if you can manage it. We always wore our shields underneath our lapels. They were little shields. I wish I had kept mine.

"I got a warrant for you, Dago Lawrence Mangano," I said. "Here, I'll read it to you."

Now, you realize, I coulda been shot right on the spot. But I took my chances that Mangano wouldn't do it. Because when I had said "Hey, Pops," he had acknowledged the greeting, confirming his identity. And within seconds after that he knew he was dealing with a government man. Messing with a government man was a serious offense. Especially on top of his other offenses. Breaking federal laws and such.

So I read the warrant, and Mangano said, "Okay, okay."

"C'mon, get in my car," I said. "Just leave yours here. Let's make it easy, no trouble."

Of course, I had a gun, too. So he knew I had him. The government didn't just send us out on these jobs. Mangano knew that. If he moved I had him covered. He knew I had a gun, and he knew I was trained to use it.

Didn't want to, but would if I had to. You don't mess with a government man. 'Cause if you do, and you muff it, you are in a lot bigger trouble. A lot! I was no Keystone Kop. Mr. Mangano knew that.

The first time his men messed with me, they didn't know who I was. Matter of fact, gangsters kill their own people sometimes. Jealousy within their own ranks. They'd rather kill one of their own men than mess with a government man. There are no consequences if they kill their own.

So Mangano got in my car. I drove him to the Federal Building, took him upstairs to the eighth floor, and brought him into the commissioner. And that was the end of the case. At least on my part.

Except that it wasn't really the end of Pops Lawrence Mangano and me. Y' see, he wasn't a bad guy really. Just a businessman who saw a way to make a quick buck off of Prohibition. He was selling liquor; that was all he was doing. Had a certain territory tied up. You had to buy from him. He headed up one of the larger districts for Capone. One of Capone's lieutenants he was, working the west side.

Later, after Prohibition was over, we became friends. Lawrence and his wife, and Babe and me. Had some good times, too. And here I had been the one who had turned him in to the commissioner. Just brought in my man. Just did my job.

Dillinger:
A Date with Destiny

NOW, THE NAME OF John Dillinger struck fear and excitement in people's minds in those days. His name, his face were all over the papers. The people's fear came from seeing how ruthless a killer he was. He would strike anywhere, kill anybody who got in his way. But there was a certain style about the man. He was tall and handsome, the ladies thought, and he dressed like a million bucks. A charmer with the ladies, that was part of his reputation. He made good press, as they say. Whenever he did somethin' it would always be written up in the papers, and it would be played up a lot, y' know. Always exaggerated, so he would look glamorous and exciting. It sold a helluva lotta papers.

He also robbed a helluva lotta banks. But John Dillinger didn't break into the crime business as a bank robber. Matter of fact, he had a very small-time start. As a young fella he started stealing cars. Just workin' on his own, he would steal a car now and then and push it off on somebody else. Sell it quick and move on. Just wanted to get some quick bucks without workin', I guess. Most people don't know this about Dillinger, that he started out as a small-time car thief.

Now, as a car thief Dillinger had a trademark that was peculiar. All his fingernails were kept nicely manicured — remember, he was fanatic about having an elegant appearance—all except his right thumb. His right thumbnail had been allowed to grow. Very long. Not the entire nail. Not all the way across, but about one-quarter of the width. The rest of the nail he kept clipped and filed and manicured. But this one part of the thumbnail had grown out real long, until it actually grew in a curve. And then the end of it had been shaped and filed so that it had a very efficient point on it. And this was his tool for breaking into cars.

Now, what kind of a strange man would want to walk around with this offensive-lookin' nail stickin' out from his hand like a spear—I mean, he could have carried any tool he wanted, or a whole array of tools, in the trunk of his car. It was peculiar. It was like an advertisement of who he was, a slap in the face to the law enforcement people everywhere he went. Like he was sayin', "Look at me. I'm the big John Dillinger! And here's my car-stealing tool right here, and you know I done it—but you can never catch me at it!"

A man like that, who flaunts his ego and his law-breaking ways in people's faces everywhere he goes, is ridin' for a fall; it's just a matter of time. And John Dillinger's time wasn't very long. His colorful career was actually pretty short.

Now, it was through his car stealing—making deals on hot cars—that Dillinger began to run into people involved in other criminal activities. And pretty soon he was offered a place among them. And before y' knew it, he was stickin' up banks.

At first he was part of a gang. But that wasn't really his style. And when he got the hang of it, he soon left the others and went out on his own. Not really a team player, Dillinger.

Now, you can't go around robbing banks without

66

arousing the wrath of the feds. Robbing banks is a federal offense. And so we were brought in on the case. Hunt down Dillinger! Stop him!

So they put out a federal warrant for him and it became the United States deputy marshal's job, under the Department of Justice, to bring him in. That meant it was our job. It fell to our office.

Capt. Hal Carr appointed Joe O'Neill, Eric Glasser, and myself to the case. Track down Dillinger! Meantime, the postal authorities had Rooney and Shanrahan on the case, because shipments of mail were involved in some of the bank robberies. Checks and things, y' know. The crooks could doctor those and turn 'em into money, too.

The postal people were in our building, so we all knew each other. The five of us worked on the case together. We made an agreement. Considering how ruthless and how agile John Dillinger was known to be, we agreed that anytime we got a tip on the guy we would tell the others, and we would all go together to confront Dillinger. Any one man against John Dillinger was not a fair match. The man would be desperate if cornered and was known to be proud of his reputation for being ruthless. He was quick to kill, a good finger man they used to say, meaning quick and on target with the trigger finger. A dangerous man. He was also known to be a slippery one. Strong and athletic, he could run fast, jump over fences, leap across rooftops, and the like. A colorful guy. Seemed to love danger, invite it.

So we went along that way, keeping to our agreement. When we got a tip, we'd pass it on; and when we could, all five of us would go out together on the tip. We went here and there. Some were phony tips; some were good tips. Now, I'm tellin' ya, bad tips are a frustration that law enforcement people have to live with. But with Dillinger even the good tips seemed to all end in frustration—because time after time he was one step, two steps ahead of us. Slippery. Real slippery.

Then one night, when we were all sittin' around in the pressroom, something happened. We used to hang out in either the pressroom or on the eighth floor of the Federal Building and play cards to pass the time. The pressroom was a good place to get leads; tips often came in there first. If a call came in, a hot tip, we could just go right out. No time was lost relaying the information. Also, no hotshot reporter could keep it to himself, losing us valuable time. So sometimes we just hung out there, especially when we were on a hot case.

So we were sittin' around playin' pinochle. Three-handed was what we liked to play. O'Neill and Glasser, Rooney and Shanrahan, and me. Three guys at a time with the cards, the other two guys sittin' around kibitzing and waitin' their turn.

So we were sittin' around shootin' the breeze and playin' a little pinochle. We hadn't noticed that Shanrahan wasn't there. He must've gotten up and moseyed out to the men's room or somethin', or maybe went to get a cup of coffee. Nobody thought anything of it. When we changed hands for the card game, we noticed Shanrahan wasn't back. We made a coupla cracks about it and got back to our pinochle. We figured he'd walk in any minute, y' know. Didn't think anything of it, really.

A little later the phone rang in the other room. It rang and rang; nobody was answering it. So O'Neill got up and went in to get the phone. A voice asked, "Hey, isn't anybody gonna do somethin' about my phone call? I can't see no action over there. Where are you guys? Is somebody on their way?" It was a tip on Dillinger.

Now, this agreement we had, that none of us should

ever go out on such a tip alone, was no light matter. Courage is one thing, but bein' a damn fool is another. Some of the characters running around tearing up Chicago in those days were just too dangerous. Chicago was no place for valor; it was a place to show good sense. We didn't want to risk losing our own men; we wanted to be certain of bringing in our target guy.

So O'Neill got the location from the caller and ran in and startled us out of our quiet game of cards. "Quick!" he shouted. "It's Dillinger! Shanrahan's gone!"

We knew instantly what had happened. Shanrahan had caught the first phone call and gone out on his own—after the most dangerous criminal of 'em all. We hadn't even realized he was gone. Obviously he had left from the other room, where the telephone was. So we scrambled. We were outa there in fifteen seconds.

The caller had said he had seen Dillinger in person. And that nobody had shown up since his first call. Now, we got an awful lotta phony tips, like I said. But in the law business you always have to treat a tip like it's for real. Every tip could be the big one.

The four of us jumped into our car and hightailed it down to the location. When we got there, it was strangely deserted, except for a garage man, an auto repair guy. We asked him if there had been any trouble, if he had seen anyone fitting either of the two descriptions; one for Dillinger, one for Shanrahan.

"Yeah," he said. "Sounds like the guy that was here a few minutes ago. He was after somebody. He ran over there. . . ." He pointed across the street and down the alley.

People had begun to emerge from nowhere, coming out of buildings, appearing magically. I guess they had all run when there was trouble and then watched from behind curtains or inside doorways. Now they were coming out.

We headed for the alley.

"There was some shootin'," the garage guy called after us.

Just then we saw a body crumpled in the alley. We were on guard. Could it be Dillinger? Maybe Shanrahan had really pulled it off. We approached cautiously. Maybe it was Dillinger lying there, and maybe he wasn't dead, just wounded. He could still be very dangerous. Then it dawned on me. And on the other guys at about the same time, I guess, because a look passed among us. The body could be our pal Shanrahan.

It was Shanrahan. He'd gotten himself slain goin' after a man who was clever and shrewd and didn't hesitate to kill. A guy who was strong and athletic and could hurtle a fence, bound across rooftops, leap over tall buildings, you name it. It just wasn't a fair match, one man against John Dillinger. Dillinger, when cornered, was as good as ten men. Ten mean men.

So Dillinger had done it again. Slipped us. And left our friend dead in an alley. Why in the heck had Shanrahan done it, gone out on the tip without us? We talked about it. Turned out Shanrahan's father was a very wealthy man, very well known in the Southwater District. That was where they sold produce; fresh fruits and vegetables. Meats and everything, too. It was the center of the food business, big business, like the market area of a big-time ranch. All the restauranteurs would buy there. Shanrahan's father was a big man in that business.

Seems Shanrahan was trying to do something on his own. Apparently his father had expected him to go into the food business. And that wasn't for Shanrahan. He could never please his father enough. Even as a grown man he kept trying to impress his father. Thought that the courage and danger of law enforcement business would somehow do it.

I didn't know all this about him before, but Rooney told us. And y' know, I could identify with that sad part of Shanrahan that didn't want to let his father down. I knew how it was to have a father who was a good person, but who had plans for your life that you just weren't comfortable with. And so you did some crazy things to try to make it right. You tried hard to prove something, and you didn't even know what it is you were trying to prove. Shanrahan had paid a helluva price.

We got other tips on Dillinger. And he kept slipping through our net. Then one particular day, when a hot tip came through, I happened to be out of the office. I had called in sick with the flu. And that was the day. A day in history. I was almost part of it. But almost doesn't count. And I've kicked myself all these years over the irony of it.

That was the day they received the tip from "the woman in red." The tip that John Dillinger would be at the Biograph Theater, 2439 North Lincoln Avenue. Accompanied by two lady friends. Dillinger would be coming out of the theater with a lady on each arm. One would be "the lady in red."

Now, everybody knew that Dillinger's girl friend liked to dress in red. But the woman who gave us the tip was not his girl friend. Not his regular girl friend. She was a friend of the girl friend, I guess. And she had some bone to pick with the authorities. A passport or visa problem, something about her status that made her afraid of being deported.

So when they had plans for the three of 'em to go to the theater, Dillinger and the girl friend and this third lady, this gal was smart enough to call in her tip as if *she* were the one who would be wearing red. This was to place the suspicion on Dillinger's well-known girl friend and not on herself. Just in case Dillinger lived through the ambush.

And so the tip that came from "the woman in red" was blamed on the girl friend and not on the other lady friend, who had really arranged the setup. It took awhile for it all to come out.

Meanwhile, I was home in bed with the flu, so I wasn't there to go out on the tip. But it was all the talk for a long time. The government men were there; they told me about it later. "We got out there and a couple of uniformed policemen came by," they said. "And they had to keep tellin' 'em, 'Get outa here. Get back! Get back!' They showed 'em our credentials and told 'em, 'Get the hell outa here!' "

Federal law enforcement credentials override the local officers' authority, y' see, so if the feds tell the policemen to get outa their way, they have to do it. 'Course the police don't want to go; they want to help. But if there isn't time to brief them, sometimes you just have to move in and take over. A big federal case like this, the feds would want to do it themselves. And they did.

Dillinger came out of the theater with the two ladies, one on each arm. And the bullets started flying. This was outside the Biograph Theater. And y' know, to this day the bullet holes are in the telegraph pole at the south end of the theater by the alley. The city council passed an ordinance that the telegraph pole never to be torn down. You can see it today; been preserved for the tourists.

A big moment in history. And I missed it—by *that much*!

The Day We
Socked It to 'Em

ONE DAY WHEN I was mindin' my own business, workin' at
my desk, in trooped a contingent from the narcotics office.
I knew all the narcotics guys, of course. At least by sight.
At least to say hello to. We all knew each other, all the
people in the building who were in the federal service.
Knew each other from when our cases overlapped, came
under more than one jurisdiction. And, too, just from
seeing each other around the building. Sure, we all knew
each other; some better, some not so well. The two I knew
best were this guy Joe and this other guy everybody called
by his last name, Bell. I didn't even know Bell's first name,
but I knew him.

So one day Joe and Bell came up to my boss and said,
"We're goin' out on a narcotics raid. Can you spare the
Hawk? We'd like to take him with us."

Now, normally we wouldn't have been involved in that
kind of operation. Not directly. That was a job for the
narcotics agents. Get the evidence, make a search, do whatever they had to do to justify a warrant. Then we'd move
in, the United States deputy marshals. We'd deliver the
warrant and bring the offenders in. Why Joe and Bell were
askin' for me I didn't know. But I wanted to go.

"Whaddya want him for?" the captain asked.

"Could be a tough one. He knows the ropes," Joe
answered.

So my boss turned and with upraised eyebrows looked questioningly at me.

I shoved my papers in the drawer and hopped to it. "Whaddya think I'm in this business for, to shuffle papers?"

They all smiled. And the captain wasn't a man to smile all that much. Everybody knew my history. How I hated duty at the IRS 'cause all it was was playin' with papers all day. They knew I had wangled a transfer to room 804 so I could see some action.

"Take him," the captain said. He had the right papers drawn up and we were off.

Now, I had never been on a narcotics raid, and I figured I might learn somethin'. That would be a plus. So it was Bell, Joe, me, and four other guys from their office. Bell and Joe and me in one car, the other four guys in another car. Joe was driving. I was ridin' in the back. We were just chewin' the fat. The others didn't volunteer to fill me in on the background dope, and I didn't ask.

Pretty soon we were over on the south side. I knew the neighborhood. Funny thing. They hadn't said where we were goin', but I could feel it comin' up. I could smell it. When you're in my kind of business, you get so you can tell when you're gettin' near somethin' that just ain't right. You can. You can smell out your prey like a hound dog.

Joe slowed down. Approached with caution, mental antennae up. At a snail's pace, we passed this little store. Looking, looking. I knew the store. It was small. Basically a grocery store, but kind of a general store as well, y' know. They had food items, of course, but they had sundries, too. Cloth, tobacco, a few clothing items, nails, hardware, a bit of everything.

"Hey, I know that place," I said.

Joe nodded and kept drivin' on. The two of 'em exchanged a look. They knew what they were lookin' for, and they saw it.

We parked a block away. Got out of the car and headed back. The other guys had parked down the street from the store and were approaching from the other direction.

"Why don't you," Bell said to me, "keep the proprietor occupied."

"The large woman?" I asked.

"That's the one. We'll look around."

"Sure."

So the three of us walked into this little store real casual, like we were customers. You had to go down a coupla steps to get in. A little below the level of the street. The other guys waited a minute, then strolled in after us.

I went up to the woman behind the counter. She was big, like a farm woman. A big, fat Italian. Lotta woman. More'n three hundred pounds if she weighed an ounce.

"I'm tryin' to find some . . . certain kind of . . . tobacco," I stammered.

Now, I just made this up. First of all, the only thing I smoked was those big cigars, which I had taken up so as to blend in with the cigar-smokin' types I had warrants on. But I wanted to occupy the woman, so I made up a fancy name of some tobacco to have somethin' to talk to her about.

"Nope. Never heard of it," she said. She was lookin' around, sort of anxious, at this sudden invasion of seven men. The narcotics agents were looking around, too.

"Well, maybe I got the name wrong," I said. "What have you got that sounds anything like it?"

Then Bell, who was in charge of the escapade, gave me the nod. I flashed the woman my credentials and whipped out the warrant from my inside breast pocket.

"Federal agents, ma'am," I said. "We have a search warrant."

She went pale. Her eyes got big. Didn't even blink.

I read her the warrant. "You understand what I just read you?" I asked.

She nodded.

"Then tell me. So I know you understand it. Correctly," I said.

She was mad. She was also afraid. Panic was reflected in her eyes, but she wouldn't show it. She just stood there.

"Please," I added. "So I know you understand it before we proceed."

Between clenched teeth she squeezed out her words. "So they can search the place," she said. She nodded over to Joe and Bell, who stood closest, then back to the others. They were hovering. Waiting.

"And . . .?" I tried to draw the words out of her.

"They claim there's narcotics here," she said. "But there ain't."

"Okay," Bell said.

Joe went over and closed the door. Turned the sign out so it said Closed. Then all of a sudden these guys were like giant ants. They were crawling all over everything in sight. Turning things over, inside out, upside down. Pulling stuff off the shelves, dumping things out of containers, peering under the counters and inside everything.

Now, I was just keepin' an eye on the woman. To make sure that she didn't make any moves. She just stood there. I wouldn't let her get to a phone or anything; that was my job.

Suddenly she reached behind herself.

"Hey," I said.

She just turned and gave me about the dirtiest look you'd ever hope to see. Pulled a little chair over and sat her massive body down on it. You wouldn't have thought that little wooden chair could hold the woman. She glared at me again.

I smiled at her. I was nice to her. We weren't rough. None of us, none of the officers. We were always nice to the people. Courteous. Unless they got rough, of course; then we had to do what we had to do.

But this woman was okay. And as far as we were concerned, she was still innocent until proven guilty. We were always careful about that.

So this search had been going on now for about half an hour, maybe forty-five minutes. And I was sort of pacin' around, taking in what was goin' on. Watching. Amazed at the places these guys thought of to look. And I was keeping an eye on the woman, too, of course. She was just sitting there in her little chair looking very smug.

I was beginning to think that if there was any evidence on the premises, these guys woulda found it by now. I headed over to Bell, still watching the woman out of one eye. Bell was over by the counter where the beans and soups were and all that sort of stuff. He was moving them all off the shelves, one by one. Shakin' the cans, to be sure it sounded like soup inside and was heavy enough to be soup.

Now, just as I got over by the counter, Bell was done with the soup cans, and he was moving on to what was next on the shelf. Bundles of socks. Bundles of white woolen socks, several pairs to a bundle, all tied together. Bell was scooping these aside, looking behind them. And one of 'em fell to the floor. But it didn't hit the floor. There behind the counter was a pail with water in it, just sittin' there. I had happened to see it because I got there and rounded the end of the counter just as the sock fell. Right into the pail.

Well, it struck me sort of funny that the bundle of socks fell right in the pail. So I looked a little closer. And saw something strange. The water was turning white—a little white cloud was spreading in it. . . .

"Bell!" I called. "Look at this. . . ."

He turned.

"Look at this! Here!" I said. "When these socks fell in here, this water got all stirred up and it's turning white."

Bell smiled. Real sly. "Hey . . ." He called the other guys over.

They came and dipped a finger in the water. Tasted it. Sure enough. It was cocaine or morphine or something. Right there in the water. And in the socks. They had been lookin' behind all the shelves, and it was right there in front of their noses. Sittin' right there on the floor in an ordinary looking pail of water.

See, what the drug dealers did was put the dope in the water; then they put these white socks in the water, too. The socks would absorb the dope along with the water. And when the socks dried out, the dope was right there in them. Didn't show 'cause the socks were white, too. So the dealers would just be selling pairs of white socks, and nobody but the addicts—the buyers—would know. So it never looked like they were passing dope. Pretty damn clever, if you ask me.

Well, that was the evidence the boys needed. And we socked it to the dealers all right. Got the woman and the others who were involved in the operation. Closed 'em down. And that was my career in narcotics.

When Is a Saloon
Not a Saloon?

PART OF MY JOB as a United States deputy marshal was to pay surprise visits wherever I found places that were illegally selling liquor—the speakeasies. With an injunction I could lock the place up, plaster federal notices around, and just plain shut down the operation. Sometimes we got official tips through the office, and sometimes we just happened onto these places in the course of our work.

Now, this one time I had been sent to a certain address on the west side of North Clark Street, in the middle of the block. I went there and hunted for the address, but there was no such number. Instead, there was a vacant lot in the middle of the block. I searched up and down the rest of the block and found nothing that resembled a saloon in any way. So I asked around.

"This address I got here is a vacant lot," I said to one guy.

He took a look at the paper with the address on it. "Yup. That's the vacant lot," he agreed.

Well, I could see it was a vacant lot. Moreover, there was no way I was gonna get any information out of these people without telling them what I was really looking for. And then the ones who knew about the speakeasy, if there was one, would be the ones who would cover it up. Worse, they would warn the owners of the place, wherever it was, and the operation would go underground until the government stopped breathing down their necks. In fact, maybe I had already tipped them off by asking about the address.

Then I figured maybe I had been given the wrong address, so I decided to check it out at the office and start over. But the office checked and double-checked for me, and they still said, "That's the address. There's supposed to be a saloon there."

I was beginning to think I was nuts. I was ready to swear that the address was nothing but an empty lot. *Did I dream I went out there?* I wondered.

So I went back and carefully checked the numbers; and sure enough, there was my empty lot where the saloon should have been. Well, clearly there was somethin' fishy goin' on.

This time I didn't ask around. I figured I'd better just smell it out. I was afraid I may already have tipped my hand too much. So I wore a hat I didn't usually wear and a little more casual outfit, just in case I ran into the guy I had questioned the last time.

I stopped by different places in the neighborhood just to listen. I figured if I were patient enough, I might just get a lead. I went into several businesses on the block and made up people to ask for or just asked questions. Just to stall around.

Now, I found a newsstand over on North Clark Street, about the 2500 block. I walked over there, bought a *Herald Examiner* for five cents, laid down a quarter, and walked away. I always bought the *Herald Examiner* 'cause they had the greatest sports writers around.

"Hey, Mister!" someone shouted.

I turned around.

"You gave me a quarter, Mister. Paper's a nickel," the newsboy said.

"Aw, forget it," I said.

Now, I knew what I was doin'. I had a plan. I walked around the neighborhood some more, memorizing places so I could sound like I belonged there. In case I needed to give the impression that I knew my way around the neighborhood. After a while I went back to the newsstand and started up a conversation with the boy. I had looked over the sports page of the paper, so I warmed him up with sports talk.

"Funny," I said, "about a week ago I met this nice lady and became better acquainted with her in a little spot where you could have a coupla beers. And now I can't seem to find the place again. I am pretty sure it was over on Clark Street, but maybe I don't remember it right. I was sorta hopin' the same lady might be there again. She seemed to know the regulars. Real nice people."

"Oh yeah," he said. "Don't worry about it. I'll show ya where it is. C'mon."

We walked over to Clark, and he pointed to a spot about two-thirds of the way down the block.

"Looks like an empty lot to me," I said.

He laughed. "Yeah, that's where it was. Now it's next door. See the coal yard? Ain't a coal yard. That's the saloon now."

"Well, thank you very much," I said. I shook his hand and headed down the block. To go calling at the coal yard saloon.

The front office was, in fact, a pretty good front. It appeared to be a legitimate coal yard operation. Out back was what appeared to be a real coal yard; I could see it through the fence that surrounded the place.

I walked into the front office, not sure how I was going to talk my way into the speakeasy, 'cause usually you had to have some kind of password. To keep people like me out. But I figured I'd play it by ear and con my way in somehow.

As luck would have it, there was nobody in the front office. I poked around, found a door that was unlocked, and let myself through. This was in the middle of the day, y' see, so they weren't expecting much business.

The door let me out the back of the office into the rear yard, where the coal business was. It was a real coal yard all right, no faking that. Or at least it had been once.

I looked around. The only thing out there besides heaps of coal was one of those temporary buildings, the portable type they put up in school yards or use sometimes for an office at a construction site.

I didn't see anybody around so I headed over to the portable building. Walked right in. And there, pretty as you please, was a speakeasy. Liquor, drinkers, and all. Oh, they were havin' a helluva time.

"Who's the boss around here?" I asked.

"Boss ain't here. I'm the bartender," said this guy, who was obviously the bartender.

"Okay. Well, I need ya to get in touch with the boss," I said.

"Boss ain't around. Sorry," he replied.

I flashed my credentials, the shield under my lapel. "United States deputy marshal," I said.

Now, that got his attention. And the attention of everybody else in there, too. They'd 'a liked to have disappeared.

I looked around at the customers. About a dozen of 'em or so. My responsibility did not include the drinkers. They were breaking the law, too, but I had no jurisdiction over them. It was the owners, the people who were dispensing the liquor illegally, who were in violation of the Volstead Act. They were the ones I had to deal with.

"There's one of two things you people can do," I said.

82

"You can either walk out or stay inside, you customers. I'm gonna lock the door. You wanna be locked in or locked out? Take your choice."

Well, now you see 'em, now you don't. I'm talking about a disappearing act. Poof—they were gone. Just the bartender and I were left.

"Okay, lock that front door," I said. "C'mon, we're gonna call your boss. I've got an injunction to close the place. Not to arrest anybody, just close the place."

We went into the side room where the phone was. It was also where they stored the merchandise. The bartender called the boss. Told him I was there and why. Then he hung up. "He'll be here," he said.

I waited. And waited. It was about an hour before the owner showed up. I would guess he'd gotten himself some advice before he came. The advice must've been that the jig was up, and that he'd better not fool around with a United States deputy marshal. He seemed like a nice enough fella. A lot of these people were just regular guys tryin' to make a buck off Prohibition.

I showed him my credentials and the injunction. He told the bartender he could go; there was no need for him to get tangled up in this. The bartender left.

"One thing I gotta ask ya," I said. "How in the hell did you move a saloon from one address to another? One day it was there at a certain address, and the next day that address was just a vacant lot. No sign that anything was ever there. You gave me a pretty good runaround."

"Easy," he said, smiling, "when you got money."

"Well, your money won't do you any good today," I said. "I'll give you time to get your personal belongings out. And then you can say good-bye. I'm lockin' up the place. For good."

He got his stuff out. He was pretty glum. Like he was

in mourning. Maybe he was just ashamed of himself, embarrassed. Like I said, he seemed like a doggone nice guy.

We went out. I locked up—put the big, heavyweight padlocks on the doors, government padlocks—and put a sign on the outside, same as the one I'd put up on the inside. Declaring that the place was under the jurisdiction of the United States federal court. It's owner walked down the steps and didn't look back.

I made my report. All about how they had turned the saloon into a vacant lot and the coal yard into a saloon. I described the people I had talked to—the newsboy, the bartender, the owner. Estimated their heights, weights, appearance, all that. Notified the local police district that we had locked up the joint, so they could keep an eye open to see if the operation sprang up somewhere else.

My job was done.

Yellow Kid Weil

NOW YELLOW KID WEIL, there was a colorful character. I'm tellin' ya, the Hollywood version of gangsters pales beside the true-life characters of that era in Chicago.

Yellow Kid earned his name. Not because he was yellow, in the manner of a coward; mind you, he was definitely not a coward. Matter of fact, he was quite bold when it came to the kinds of deals he dared to undertake. He was a lawyer himself; yet he laughed at the law and the government. He knew the ins and outs of the law, and he knew how to get around it. He knew how to make it hard to catch him.

Everyone knew Weil was up to mischievous deals; he had quite a public reputation for that. He made no effort to maintain a low profile, as they say. Rather, he flaunted himself in defiance of law and public opinion. He loved the recognition. Went out of his way to call attention to himself. No sneaky and secretive man would have created the image he did. No, the Yellow Kid's name definitely did not mean he was cowardly yellow. He earned that name from the flashy image he struck.

The Kid surrounded himself with the color gold. Everything he had was in a shade of gold. His car was the most beautiful vehicle you'd ever hope to see. A huge Packard convertible, shiny, gold-colored. Now, I don't suppose there's many people around anymore who remember those old Packards, but it was a very grand automobile. A Packard was like a yacht on wheels. Huge and very elegant.

As you might guess, Yellow Kid Weil's gold Packard convertible had all gold fittings. Polished gold door handles. Gold dash, Gold trim. Everything gold. Even the seats were a light, creamy gold color.

The man even dressed in shades of gold. Wore light-colored, creamy yellow or goldish-tan outfits. Three-piece suits. All imported. Had a gold watch chain, gold-toned light fedora hat, cream-colored shoes. Even his red hair had a glint of gold highlights in it, and he sported a mustache and little goatee. The Kid was a very distinguished-lookin' gentleman, down to his perfect manicure. Everything about him was impeccable. What a picture.

People used to watch for the Kid to come down the street. It was quite a show. He'd be driving his big gold convertible and not only would he be all decked out in gold himself but his lady friends would be, too. They had to fit in with his image or Weil didn't bother with 'em.

He was a real charmer. Only stood about five foot four and couldn't 'a weighed more than a hundred thirty or so. But a good-lookin' guy. About fifty or fifty-five years old around the time I saw him. Now, that was considered elderly at the time. Folks didn't live as long then as they do now. But he looked good. And with his money and his looks that man could woo any woman. Mostly he was seen with some fancy countess or beautiful actress, people like that.

Now, what Yellow Kid Weil was up to was this. He went over to England—traveled around other parts of Europe, too, but mostly England—to round up investors for certain stocks and bonds. The man was such a charmer he could have sold ice cubes to Eskimos. Now, he had already sold some of his stocks and bonds in America before he went to Europe, and he made a killing on them there, especially in England. He took in a couple of million bucks of investors' money. And a couple of million bucks wasn't peanuts; it was some haul in those days. Only problem was, it was all a scam. Phony stocks, phony bonds. Big-time embezzlement.

So when he got back to the States, there was a warrant out for his arrest. And that's where I came in. I was given the warrant.

I tried to catch up with the man, tracking him at every haunt he was known to frequent. But he always seemed to be one jump ahead of me. I had other cases I was workin' on at the same time, so I couldn't always be where he might be.

Then one day I was over on the northeast side of Chicago, workin' another case, and I was walkin' past a bank on the corner of Broadway and Racine. Walkin' south on Broadway. It's still very clear in my mind. And there was his car. Now, I had never seen Yellow Kid Weil's car before, but I knew it when I saw it. That car was famous.

I looked around. Didn't see anybody of particular interest. *Well*, I thought, *I think I'll just hang around a while. See who turns up.*

For a while I just walked up and down the block or stood in the doorway of a building next to the Kid's car, all the time looking around. Then on one of my walks down the block, I had turned to walk back when, sure enough, there was Yellow Kid himself coming out of the bank. Three other people were with him.

Now, the Kid was dressed up real flashy, as befitted his reputation. Tweed suit, sort of a golden tan. Beautiful. Three-piece suit, vest and all. Light fedora hat. Gold watch chain flashing in the sun. Oh yeah, there was no mistaking the man. It was Yellow Kid Weil all right. And three people with him. A tall lady on his arm and another couple. Trouble was, he had his car right there in front of the bank, and I was clear down the block. In a minute or two he'd be gone. Right out from under me.

So I took off on the double. I got to him just as he was opening the car door for his lady friend. The other two were already in the back.

The Kid's lady friend was very distinguished looking. Carried herself like a queen or somethin'. Turned out to be a real countess, I found out later. Oh, she was elegant. Wrapped in furs and all. She had a hat on, so I didn't get much of a look at her face. Y' know, the kind of hat they used to wear then, with a little veil hanging down in front. She was no spring chicken, though. Forty, maybe forty-five, I'd guess. But some fancy company for the Kid to be keeping.

The other man with him I recognized. A Mr. Bradstreet, well known around Chicago in those days. And he had a lady friend with him.

Yellow Kid Weil was holding the door. I slowed down as I neared them. Didn't want to call attention to myself running at them. So I sauntered up to him just as he was holding the door open for the countess, and I said, "Just a minute, sir."

They stood there just looking at me for a moment, so I seized the opportunity and, hopping right into the car, sat down.

"Who the hell are you?" the Kid asked.

"Well, how's everything?" I asked in reply.

"What the hell is goin' on?" he queried again.

"Aw, you won't object to this," I said. I pulled out my credentials and flashed the badge under my lapel. "I'm United States Deputy Marshal Lee Tashjian. I have a warrant for your arrest. Here, I'll read the warrant to you . . ." I pulled it out of my inside breast pocket and read it to him. Lucky for me I had a habit of always carrying with me the several warrants assigned to me, because you never know when something might develop. Good thing, 'cause this was one of those times when I woulda kicked myself if I hadn't had the necessary paperwork with me.

The Kid just stood there, calm as could be. Now that he knew who I was and what the intrusion was all about, he wasn't ruffled a bit. I guess he was confident he could beat the rap.

"Now, we'll have to follow the regular procedure," I said. "And that means we go straight to the Federal Building. Do you want to go in your car, or do you want me to call a police escort from the Summerdale Police Station?"

"No, no. No need to do that," he said.

So we drove down to the Federal Building in his car. And I don't mind tellin' ya, it was an exciting little adventure for me. Everybody on the streets turned and looked at that car goin' by. Now, Yellow Kid Weil may have grown accustomed to all that attention, but for me, a young whippersnapper of a United States deputy marshal, it was a thrill.

Wonder if I'll ever have a car like this? I wondered to myself. And y' know what? I've got a great big gold car sittin' out in front of my house right now. And it's mine. And I feel pretty good drivin' it, too.

Well, we got down to the Federal Building, me and Yellow Kid and his pals. It was a silent trip, I'll tell you that. Nobody said nothin'. What was there to say?

Now, we got down there and I wondered what in the heck I was supposed to do with the other three? Here I had all these people on my hands, and I was interested in just the one. Couldn't drag 'em all into the Federal Building and make 'em sit around while we questioned the person we had a warrant for. Could hardly have left 'em standin' in the street either.

Well, the government kept some nice rooms in a hotel across the street from the Federal Building for just such occasions as this. So we parked the car and I put a ticket on it stating that it was in the possession of a United States deputy marshal. And I took 'em all into the hotel across the street from the Federal Building and checked 'em into a couple of nice rooms.

Now, Yellow Kid Weil said he'd like a few minutes to freshen up. The man looked like he'd just stepped of the front of a men's fashion magazine and yet he wanted to freshen up. I figured he was gonna call his lawyer. But what the heck.

So I left 'em in the rooms and went to call my partner, Eric Glasser. Now, I knew that Yellow Kid Weil was too smart to skip out on a federal warrant, still I stuck around to keep an eye open.

My partner arrived and we waited. The Kid didn't come down for a couple of hours. No big deal to me. It wasn't my job to treat the man as if he were in jail. A warrant was only the beginning of a case. He hadn't been proven guilty of anything at that point.

When the Kid finally came downstairs, my partner and I escorted him across the street and upstairs to the United States Commissioner Henry C. Beitler. We left him there; now he was out of our hands.

I followed his case with great interest, of course. It turned out they set his bond at a neat one hundred thousand dollars. He spoke in his own defense at this stage of the proceedings. He was a lawyer himself, y' know, and didn't need professional representation although he had been disbarred. And he got the commissioner to reduce the bond to twenty-five thousand. Then he called a bail bondsman—whose job it was to supply 10 percent of the bond in cash—and out he walked. Free on bail.

The case finally came up for a hearing. It was held on the fifth floor right there in the Federal Building, so I thought, *Well, I'll just go in there and see what's goin' on.*

It was a circus. The prosecution had plenty of charges against the Kid. Offenses I didn't even know about. But he was a slippery one, and he and his attorneys sang and danced their way around every accusation. By the time it was over, Yellow Kid Weil had been declared not guilty on every charge. He walked out a free man. Some travesty of justice, I'll say that.

Soon after that the Kid bought a big hotel on the corner of Windsor and Sheridan roads in Chicago. About six stories high. Nice place. A pretty good-sized chunk of money he had fleeced from people in England, as well as in the United States, went into it.

We still watched for his car to go by. The man was somethin' to see. Bigger than life.

How My Reputation Was Nearly Lost in the Ashcan

NOW, FOR A WHILE, a big scandal had been going on regarding narcotics, and I had been assigned to stake out a certain case. Also about this time I had been breaking in Eric Glasser, who was new to room 804; he was going to be my partner.

This narcotics stakeout was the first case we were on together. So, of course, I figured I was gonna show him the ropes, y' know, show him how it was done.

The warrant was for some woman who had been under surveillance with regard to narcotics. I was supposed to keep an eye on a certain building until I could see her either coming or going. Then I was supposed to serve the warrant on her.

So I took my new partner with me, green as he was, and we went over to the west side and located the building this woman was supposed to frequent. She had been seen comin' and goin' at night. So we went out there in the evening, thinking to catch her right off. But in case she didn't come by that first night, we were ready to hold out through the next day and catch her the second night.

The building was easy to find; it was the only two-story building on the block. But we were surprised to find it looking deserted. Like nobody lived there at all. Completely dark.

Now this seemed strange to us. We had figured it was

a drop-off and pickup spot for narcotics. We hadn't thought about it being an abandoned building. Why would a woman come and go, alone, to a dark deserted building in the night? Even for a narcotics deal. There were safer ways to do it. But it was the building, all right.

Well, we were in for a long watch. We got there when it was already night. Lights were on in the neighboring buildings, but not a single sign of life showed in our building.

I'm tellin' ya, the whole thing was peculiar from the start. But we had our assignment, so we staked out the place. We didn't want to sit in the car and wait 'cause that makes you look suspicious. So we started out by walkin' up and down the street a couple of times. We were afraid if we walked all the way around the block we might miss her. Then, after a while, we found ourselves a pretty good spot in an empty lot, across the way and down a bit. A few hundred feet or so from the building. Maybe a thousand feet.

And it got later and later. Pretty soon nobody was on the street; everything was quiet and still—it was the middle of the damn night! And nothing had happened at all. There was no sign that anybody lived in the building or came or went to make drug deals. Nothin'.

Now, Eric and I each had a little flask of brandy in a pocket, to keep us warm in case the stakeout went on into the night and it got cold. Well, it sure did that. Went on into the night *and* got cold. We were mighty glad we had packed our little provisions.

So we were just sippin' our brandy and shootin' the breeze and watchin' a dark building. We had made a little place for ourselves in the empty lot. On the ground, with a fence to lean on. We could see, but we wouldn't be noticed particularly. We figured we looked like just a couple of guys from the neighborhood, hangin' out. We had dressed very inconspicuously, of course, so we wouldn't arouse any particular notice.

Well, time was passin' by and nothin' was happening. So finally, around two or three in the morning, I said, "Hey, let's take shifts watchin' this place. It looks like this could be a wild-goose chase; no sense in our both stayin' up all night watchin' nothin'. You get a little shut-eye; then I'll wake you up and you can watch for a while."

So we took turns. One watchin' and the other free to doze off. Well, stretched out in this field, we musta looked like a coupla winos, sippin' our brandy and dozin' off. And nothin' ever happened all night long. Or the whole next day, either. Or the following night. But, y' see, we wouldn't leave our post for anything but the most essential things. We had been assigned to bring in this suspect, and we couldn't take a chance on missing her.

So one of us would stay on watch, while the other went to get some sandwiches or somethin'. And now and then we'd move the car from one place to another. Around the block or up the street, so the car wouldn't begin to draw suspicion.

Now, this went on for three nights and three days! And we musta looked like the worst of the winos by now—clothes all crumpled, and the two of us just hangin' around this empty lot! Seventy-two hours! We were beginning to talk mutiny. Were mighty close to throwin' in the towel.

It was movin' in on the fourth night of watch. We were dog-tired. And bored beyond description. Now, y' remember, I had gotten myself into this business because I wanted excitement. The IRS was too flat. Me, I wanted excitement. Well, at this point, sittin' behind a desk shufflin' IRS papers looked pretty exciting.

And suddenly, there she was! Out of nowhere. A shadowy slip of a figure appeared, and—poof, she was inside the door and gone. Then, upstairs, a light went on.

Well, we, quick, leaped to our feet, and we started brushing the wrinkles out of our clothes and running our hands through our hair—and we started laughin'. Damned if we weren't awful lookin'.

But duty called and United States deputy marshals respond—and we were off! Crossed the street. Went up the front steps. Rang the doorbell. Nothin'. Now we knew she was in there. So we looked at each other, and I motioned to Eric to go around the back. I waited long enough to give him time to get back there. Then I tried the door. It wasn't even locked.

I went in. And met Eric comin' in through the rear entrance. At the bottom of the stairs, I called out, "United States deputy marshals," and we marched right up.

And there she was. A slender woman, maybe thirty-five or so, dressed in a plain black dress, black shoes. *Yeah,* I thought, *makes it nice and easy to slip in and out of a building at night.* We figured her contact would probably be here soon. And would probably be scared off by our voices. But that was no concern of ours. We had a warrant for the woman and we would bring her in.

Now, she was just standin' there lookin' as guilty as you please. With the evidence right there in her hands. So we flashed the badges that were under our rumpled lapels, and I said, "United States Deputy marshals Tashjian and Glasser. We have a warrant for your arrest, ma'am. And to search the premises."

The woman just stood there. Never moved. I nodded to Eric to take the evidence from her hands. She was holding a brown box. And whatever was in that container, we wanted it.

I pulled out the warrant and held it out to her. Recited her rights, read her the contents of the warrant. Eric took the container, set it aside, and stood between her and the container. We had to get her to sign the papers. Now it seemed like that might be a problem. She was like one of those dress store mannequins. She never moved. Maybe she was in a drugged state herself, I figured. Her eyes just looked at us, but she never moved.

Well, with a little gentle urging I got her to sign her name on the papers, and we did a quick search around the place and found nothin'. There was nothin' to find, no place to search. The house was empty. It was as deserted as it looked from the outside.

Then we took the container and sealed it up. We both put our initials on it, and we asked her to initial it too, which she did. All this was to validate that we had not messed with the container or its contents, so that whatever was in the container when we got it down to the authorities would be exactly what was in it when we first found it.

We told the woman we would have to take her in to the Federal Building, pending investigation. Still she never said a word. So we escorted her out with us and headed up the street. I leaned over to Eric and asked, in an aside to him, "Where'd you put the car?"

He had to think. We had moved it so many times then we weren't sure where it was. He nodded to the right. We got to the end of the block and looked right. There was the car. Eric smiled. I knew he hadn't been sure it would be there.

The three of us got in the car, the suspect between us. We went down to the Federal Building to turn over both the evidence and the suspect to the commissioner. Oh, we were proud of ourselves. The long sting—seventy-two hours—at our hardship post had paid off.

So we were sittin' there all smug while the commissioner opened the container. Inside the brown box was a small black tin. And inside the tin was a sort of powder. But it was dark powder instead of the white we had expected to see. The commissioner asked the woman, "What is this?"

"The ashes of my husband," she said. That was the first she had spoken!

The commissioner sent the contents to the lab to be analyzed. The report came back. Ashes of deceased.

On being questioned, the woman revealed that her husband had died recently of cancer. His final days had been very painful, and he had been smoking opium to ease the pain. Apparently someone had reported that the woman had been making buys of opium, and the path had led to this. A fright to add to her sadness. She told us that she and her husband had once lived in the house, when he was healthy and they were happy, and now she returned there with his ashes to meditate and remember.

Of course. The black dress. The poor woman was in mourning. Mrs. Rose McConnell. I will never forget her name.

We apologized. But it wasn't enough. The case made the papers. Oh, they had a heyday with it. Thought it was very funny. Ran a picture of Mrs. McConnell sitting, holding the box of her husband's ashes. And me, the deputy marshal who had taken her into custody. Some days it just doesn't pay to get outa bed.

The Plunge of Dr. Price

SOMETIMES IT SEEMS as if there are signs hinting to us about the future, warnings, if only we could read them. It seems like that now, looking back on this certain case with this famous doctor. If I could've read the signs, I might've been more on guard for what was to happen soon in my own life. If only I could've stood at the shoulder of Fate and read the cards in his hands, well, my whole life might have turned out different.

This doctor, by the name of Price, nearly plunged to his death in an act that occurred in less than a minute. And not long after that, my own career plunged to a premature death because of an act that occurred in less than a minute. The difference was, I had nobody there to save me. At least, not in time.

This one started out like a routine case. Well, not really routine. He was a well-known physician in the city of Chicago, and I can't say we had well-known physicians in the tank on drug charges every day. But this man had gotten himself mixed up pretty bad with drugs. Selling them and taking them himself, too.

Doctors have a very high rate of drug addiction, y' know. To this day, it's a fact. Probably even worse now than it was in those days, what with all the new drugs that've been discovered or invented in the meantime. Doctors have access to all the drugs, so it's easy for them to get started, and easy, to, for them to get away with it. At least, they think so when they start. Until they get caught in their own trap.

Now, this Dr. Price was into the drug business pretty deeply. And it was a police informer who ratted on him. Tipped off the narcotics boys. They'd been trying to close in on this guy for weeks without knowing the real identity of who it was they were after. And without knowing the pattern of his movements clearly enough to nail him.

Now, just when they had begun to get close, one of the doctor's buyers tipped off the agents in exchange for protection from prosecution himself. That's the way drug dealers are, y' know. They'll rat on their best friend if they think they can save their own skin. There's no loyalty among 'em; they can't trust each other long enough to blink their eyes.

Anyway, the narcotics boys had their lead, so they set the guy up. But they still didn't know he was this famous doctor. They set up a purchase, a delivery deal, over on Jackson Boulevard. This poor Dr. Price wasn't really shrewd enough to slip away from professional, law enforcement people. He was a very proper doctor, not a streetwise guy. A sitting duck up against the pros.

Well, they set him up, caught him in the act delivering the merchandise. Roy Falk and William Frade were the guys that caught him. I knew 'em both. They brought him in, put him in a cell up on the eighth floor of the Federal Building, and locked him up. Routine.

Anyway, I guess it was all too much for the doctor to bear. The man was a mess. His drug habit had really taken its toll. He looked sick, and he was definitely not able to think clearly. He was a slave to the drugs; he had committed criminal acts in providing and selling illegal drugs to others; and it was certain he would be thrown out of the medical profession. Then there was the humiliation he was bringing to his family. And that was enough to break any man. How could he support his family if he couldn't practice as a doctor anymore? And how could he face them, or his former colleagues, or his friends? Or, most of all, himself. Well, you add all that up, and it isn't hard to understand that the man was desperate.

So there he was in a cell up on the eighth floor of the Federal Building, and he was just sitting there with his head drooped over. I saw him and wondered if he was dozing off or what. Or if he was about to be sick.

For some reason—I don't remember why exactly—the agents came in and began transferring the man to another cell. I was aware of it. I was in the same room, but I wasn't involved directly. Then, suddenly, the doctor made a dash for it—away from the agents who were escorting him.

Now, with my history and training, it was in my bones to act on reflex, quicker than you could think about it. Especially if you sensed danger in the situation. You learn that. You learn to react before there's time to think. Too often you don't have that time; you'd be dead before you had finished a thought. And in that moment, when this guy leaped away from the agents who were around him, there was no way to know what he might do.

Instinctively, I jumped up and intercepted him, pinning him down. Me, the littlest guy in the room. While he had eluded a whole handful of bigger, burlier guys. I must've jumped halfway across the room in an instant. Faster than a speeding bullet, that was me. I pounced on him, just in time to restrain him—before he could dive right out the window! Now remember, this was eight stories up. Yeah, what he had in mind was to end it all. Another split second and it woulda been too late.

There was a quick scuffle, and the surrounding agents hustled the man back into his cell. Then, while they were locking him up, damned if he didn't grab the gun from a guard and try to shoot himself! That's what I call determined. He meant business, I'll tell you that.

Now, it was written up in all the papers how I saved the doctor's life. I was a hero for a day. But y' know what? I never heard the end of the story. I've always wondered, all these years, what became of that man. Did he try again and succeed in killing himself—or did he make it through the rehabilitation program? Did he get things back in balance? Did he go home to his family, rebuild his life?

Well, that was one of the peculiar things about the kind of job I had. Sometimes you never knew the ending. When you save a man's life, you have a strange link to that person. You have a need to know if his was a life worth saving. You want good to come into his life. You hope that, in the final analysis, you were fated to save his life for a better purpose.

But—you may never know.

The Brawl in the Hall

NOW, Y' GOTTA UNDERSTAND that the guys we brought in for violating the Volstead Act—that is, dealing in liquor, whether they were makin' it or sellin' it—were, for the most part, just regular guys, not real criminals. I mean they didn't have a record of robberies or murders or anything like that; they weren't big gang-type criminals, most of 'em. They were guys, just tryin' to make a buck on Prohibition. And when we apprehended 'em and brought 'em in and filed criminal charges against 'em they could be pretty unpredictable.

Here would be a regular nice guy, just doin' some deals on the side to make a buck, and suddenly he was labeled a criminal in the eyes of the federal government—it could change his life drastically, in a very negative way, havin' this kind of thing on his record. Forever. He might pull a gun; he might do anything—he was fightin' for his life. You just never knew what they might try.

A case in point.

Tony Cantenza owned a nice little restaurant over on South State Street. Now, Tony was a nice guy; we all knew him. Unfortunately, he had been brought in for servin' liquor. So until the hearing we had him in custody in the holding cell on the eighth floor of the Federal Building. The hearing was right there in the Federal Building, too.

Now, it came out at the hearing that Jake Marsh, one of our Prohibition agents, had gone into Tony's place and sat around a little while shootin' the breeze; then, appar-

102

ently, he'd gotten a headache, stomachache, whatever. So, looking a little under the weather, he mentioned that he wasn't feeling so good.

And guess what? Tony himself said, "Here, I'll fix ya a little somethin' to pick ya up." And he handed Jake a glass of whiskey!

Nice guy. Just bein' hospitable to a pal, right? And he got nailed for it. Jake, of course, had to bring him in.

When all this came out at the hearing, Jake Marsh said right there in front of everybody, that he had "feigned illness." Now, Tony and his attorney, a man by the name of Col. John V. Clinnin, got all riled up. Understandably enough. But they were reprimanded by the court, and they restrained themselves, knowing it would not go well for them if they caused a ruckus during the hearing. They were still hoping to get Tony off.

Tony got indicted, however.

The hearing over, everybody filed out into the hall. Tony and the colonel were about to bust with anger. Now, this colonel fella was not the type of guy you would want to pick a fight with. He was a big man, weighin' in at maybe two hundred sixty pounds. Besides that, he was a mean sort, an intimidating type. Not a polite gentlemen.

Out in the hall the colonel grabbed hold of Jake Marsh by the collar, backed him up against the wall, and yelled, "It was a sting! . . . You sonofabitch! It was a put-up job! A straightaway entrapment! You goddam government bastards are usin' illegal means to do yer dirty work! I'll give ya a taste of illegal means."

Now, Jake Marsh was no pansy, but bein' face to face with a fist the size of a football is not a pleasant way to wrap up business. He denied the accusation, but everybody there had heard him admit to the court it was a "feigned illness," so what good was it to deny it now.

The colonel was mad. And he was about to level some mean blow on Marsh. And Tony was right there behind him, dancin' around with anger, just itchin' to get into the fray. And there were about half a dozen United States government officials right there—Charles Vursell, chief prohibition officer of the department; George Carmichael, assistant United States attorney; and, of course, me.

The others were holding back, hesitating to turn it into a fight. But me, I jumped right into it. Quick as a flash, I leaped over to this colonel fella and intercepted the fist that was pullin' back ready to rearrange Jake Marsh's face. Now, the colonel was a big man, like I said, and I could hardly get the scale up to one hundred thirty, soakin' wet. I guess it musta looked pretty comical. A little bantam rooster takin' after the prize bull. But the colonel backed down. I musta looked mad, which I was. You don't mess up a federal agent when I'm around.

In that moment, while these guys stood there stunned—me with my fist pulled back like I was about to deliver a punch that would take the colonel fella halfway to kingdom come—the commissioner, seeing all this from down the hall, called out real loud, "Marshal! Put everyone involved in this squabble under arrest! Immediately!"

Now me, I was the only marshal present.

They all looked at me. I wasn't afraid for one moment to take on this bruiser of a fella. And they knew I meant business. And poof—they were gone! They dispersed in the blink of an eye. Very orderly, I must say. Now you see 'em, now you don't.

Well, the papers made a fuss over it. "The miniature United States marshal," they called me. Now I'm gonna tell ya, because I am the living proof of this, physical stature doesn't have much to do with real strength. That comes from inside. If you're strong inside, nobody can stop ya.

You can bet your life on it. I did, many times. And I'm still here to talk about it.

On a Dark and Rainy Night

I HAD A WARRANT out for a man; been hunting him down for days. Along with some others on my list. I carried the warrant with me, always on the lookout for this guy, but takin' care of my other business at the same time, y' know.

And one day out of Niles Center I saw the man come out of his house and—pow! I knew it was my man. Description fit, everything. I knew it was his neighborhood, knew he should be there sometime. And there he was. Right on time. I had gotten pieces of information from around the neighborhood, y' know. But carefully. You gotta be careful that you don't arouse too much interest when you start pokin' around.

Now, this man was involved in making counterfeit stamps for the whiskey bottles. And on the side he was also sellin' whiskey by the bottle. Whiskey and counterfeit stamps. We thought he was just small time, even though he turned out to have a bigger operation than we knew. Turned out he was the one sellin' counterfeit labels all over Cook County. Even if he was small time, still it was illegal to be makin' money off the forbidden booze business. We woulda been after him anyway.

So this guy's business was pretty much under cover; in fact, I don't even think his neighbors knew what he was up to. Makin' his own whiskey, addin' the color and the alcohol, just like the big boys, but his whiskey-makin' operation was a small operation. Goin' on there in his own place. Big beautiful house. Had the appearance of a very respectable, well-to-do citizen. He knew what he was doin' though. He knew the booze and labels business. Made his counterfeit labels to order. Sold to all the big boys.

So there he was, coming out of this very elegant house, and he jumped in his big fancy car and took off. Lotta money around in those days. The people who had money, they had a lot of it.

Well, I was ready for him. I took off after him. It was evening, dark and cold and sort of misty. Like it wanted to rain. It was tryin' to rain, but it wasn't rainin' yet. Y' know, the pavement was slick with little needles of drizzle, but you couldn't see it comin' down, it was too fine. Just looked misty.

Well, this guy was very nervous about someone tailin' him, that was clear. He took off like a jackrabbit. I mean he went skiterin' around those residential streets like he'd got fleas. He knew every turn in the road, like his car was anchored onto a trolley track. And I was on his tail.

We came barrelin' out on Milwaukee Avenue. Lawrence and Milwaukee. It was pourin' down rain now, not just buckets—barrels. And he was sure he was bein' chased, no doubt about that. He musta thought I was somebody from the mob 'cause this man was runnin' for his life, and all of a sudden—around the corner, an S turn—I went into a swerve. With rain pourin' down on the slick road, my car couldn't hold onto the pavement; I was twistin', my car going sideways in the street, fast—then I saw this lamp post crammin' itself right up into my face, and I was goin' through the windshield.

I woke up in the hospital, but I could hardly feel anything. Couldn't think clearly. Couldn't talk. They'd got me wrapped up like a mummy. Eighty-seven stitches in my head. All in the neck and the head. Came within a hair's breadth of cutting the jugular vein. I was caught dangling halfway through the windshield. Death breathing on me. *That close* to slicing the jugular. Now, the jugular is the vein in your neck that carries the blood back from your head to your heart, y' know. You cut that and you're gone before you can say good-bye. I shoulda died. That's what they said, I shoulda died.

Well, they musta got to me in a damn hurry; course I never remembered any of that. They rushed me to the hospital and went out to get my wife. Four o'clock in the morning. They knew who I was. My ID was on me, my United States deputy marshal's badge, all that.

They had come to the house to get her at about four o'clock in the morning. In the pourin' down rain, they came to the house and woke up this young pregnant wife with the news that her husband wasn't gonna make it through the night.

But Babe had the two little girls asleep, and she was pregnant with another one and couldn't just leave in the middle of the night. Had to wait till morning when she could have someone stay with the girls. And I might have been dead by then. That's what they told her. They expected me to be dead within seventy-two hours.

Well, I made it to morning, you already know that. So Babe came to the hospital and she was tryin' to find me. They told her the room, and she looked in and then went back to the nurse and said, "No, that's not him. Where is he?" Course, she was afraid I was already dead.

Nurse told her the same room. She went back, looked again. Three times she looked and didn't even recognize me, they'd got me wrapped up so much and what was left of my face was so swollen and distorted. The only spaces in the mummy suit were the eyes and mouth, and they were not much like the old Lee. She had no idea it was me. Poor Babe, she thought I had died in the night, and they had put somebody else in the bed.

So she went out in the lobby again. "He's not in there!" she cried. "Please! You've got to find my husband! He's been in an accident, and I've got to see him!"

Finally they brought her to the room and said it was really me. Showed her on the chart at the foot of the bed. She came up close. Looked, tryin' to find me in all those bandages, behind the swelling and the bruises and the slashed remains of the face of her husband. Yes, it was me. She didn't wanta believe it.

Now, to hear Babe tell it, she'll tell ya I was some good-lookin' sonofabitch before that.

I still carry the scars; you can see 'em today. You gotta look pretty close now, of course. I'm nearly ninety-two now; quite a few years have passed by. I was in my twenties then. But the scars are still with me; they tell the story. Up my face and down—face was split wide open. Across my nose all the way to my ear. Across the forehead. And two big gashes on top of my head. Went right through the damn windshield. Right through. Musta been somethin' to see it. Got a lopsided head now. Coupla bumps upon the top of my head that have never gone away. They're from the skull fracture.

Poor Babe. She was terribly upset. There she was — pregnant —and they told her they expected me to die any minute. What a thing to tell a sweet young wife, with two little babies and a third one on the way.

Now, Babe was used to the danger of my job. At least she thought she was. She knew every time I walked out the door I might not come back alive. But it's different when it really happens. Or when it comes that close. You think you're ready, but you're not.

Babe used to say she never expected it to happen with

an accident like that. She figured maybe I'd get shot or maybe I'd just disappear. But she wasn't ready for the grisly sight of her husband all torn up. Car accidents are the kind of thing that happen to regular people, y' know; you don't have to be a United States deputy marshal to get in a car accident! She just wasn't ready for it.

Well, it was a coupla months before I could get back on my feet, get back to work. My man had made quite a getaway. I was back to square one on that case. At least he wouldn't recognize me now. But the car he would.

So I dug out the warrant and went out after him again. I absolutely insisted that nobody else in the service could go after my man. There was a premium on this one, y' see. I had already made a down payment on this particular catch. This man was mine. And I got him, all right. Had a lot of satisfaction bringin' that one in.

But when our baby was born, our third girl, she was lacking sufficient body fluid. The baby's condition was traced back to the shock Babe went through at the time of my accident. The baby was in the hospital six weeks, on the edge of death herself. Just a tiny little thing, clinging to a promise of life. Such a fragile little thing.

Finally we got to bring her home. Five weeks we'd had her. Our oldest daughter, Laverne, was about five years old then. Laverne had a little cold, as children often do it seems. Now, Laverne thought the baby was a little doll. Not really a doll, but she thought of her as a pretty plaything. The baby only weighed five pounds and two ounces. So tiny.

Laverne wanted to hold the baby. Now, we were young ourselves; Babe was only seventeen when we got married. And people didn't know then all the things they know now about health and babies and all. We lived life more simply. We did what we did. We didn't question everything.

110

So Babe let Laverne hold the baby. And Laverne sneezed. It must've been more germs than the fragile little baby could handle. She had had such a struggle to live, and she was still weak. Our little baby got pneumonia. And we lost her.

Y' know, that was too high a price to pay for the job I had. I believed in the importance of my work, bringing in lawbreakers. But that was too high a price.

The Burglar Club, the Woman's Christian Temperance Union, and the Spikes of Evanston

NOW, THERE WAS THIS Marbinson Drugstore over on Irving Park Boulevard. And somehow or other I got wind of some inside information that these folks were selling liquor on the sly, y' know, to people they knew. Using a legitimate drugstore business as a front. Well, they couldn't get away with that too long. Not with the Prohibition law, and not with deputy marshals around to enforce it.

So I did what I had to do, and I got the place closed down. Caught 'em red-handed. Had an injunction put on the place, and they had to shut down their whole business, drugstore and all. At least, till there could be a hearing and the whole thing set straight. It was all pretty routine up to that point.

Well, I had a certain pride in my work. And I figured that the places I closed down represented my doin' my job and doin' it well. And you don't go messin' with a man of pride.

From time to time I always kinda checked back on my cases, tried to find out how they turned out, y' know. Well, this one made me mad 'cause I heard that a band of burglars was using that shutdown drugstore of mine for a meeting hall! And that they were still carryin' on the liquor business! Now, you can bet I took this as a personal affront

112

to me, an honorable man in the government service, and the one who had closed the place down.

So I went out there. You bet. I had pictures in my head of these guys sittin' around in that drugstore just carryin' on a swell liquor business and laughin' at what they were gettin' away with. I didn't like 'em laughin' at the government, and I didn't like 'em laughin' at me. I had it in mind to show 'em that it wasn't so funny.

So I sniffed around there for days. Actually, mostly nights. Sometimes I just cruised by in my car, checking up. Seein' if there was anything unusual goin' on. Lettin' the neighborhood folks get used to seein' me around, so they wouldn't think nothin' of it. Then sometimes I'd park some blocks away and take a walk. Just strollin' around the neighborhood like I was out for a breath of fresh air, y' know.

Then, sure enough, one evening along came these guys, in ones and twos and threes, goin' into the drugstore by the back way. Walked right past the injunction notice like it wasn't there. And on top o' that, some of 'em were carrying cases of what I knew had to be whiskey. *Boy*, I thought, *I'm gonna get 'em, and I'm gonna get 'em good.*

So I waited till they stopped comin'. Figured I might as well catch as many guys in there as possible. Besides, I was curious myself just how big this operation was. There was a bunch of 'em all right.

Well, they dribbled in a few at a time, and finally there were no more arriving at the party. It was time for me to carry out my own personal raid.

I walked right in, and there they were, like sitting ducks. I flashed my badge, showed my credentials, announced my intentions. And suddenly these guys weren't laughin' anymore.

Found ninety-eight pints of whiskey, a bottle of gin, a bottle of pure alcohol, and two gallons of wine. The

113

current assets of the Burglar Club. Right there on the premises. With the injunction tacked right there on the door in plain sight. I didn't hang 'em; they hung themselves. I was doin' my job.

This time I got 'em not only closed down but nailed up. I mean literally. I went out there and nailed the place shut. You don't get the last laugh on the Hawk.

Now, speaking of nailing a place shut, that brings to mind my most famous nail job. It was out in Evanston. Now, I have to tell ya how Evanston fit into the whole subject of the ban on liquor. Evanston was, I'm afraid, the borning place of Prohibition itself.

It seems that the Woman's Christian Temperance Union out in Evanston was especially excited—in a very negative way—about the idea of people drinking. And they had tried and tried to get the government or the public or somebody to listen to 'em. They jumped up and down, sang out terrible warnings of hell and damnation, and tried to get votes taken, but nobody was listening. They made a few ripples from time to time but never any real waves, y' know what I mean?

Now, when the boys went away to war, that was a different thing. I'm talkin' about the big war, World War One, the war we really believed would be the end of all wars. While all our boys were over in Europe fighting for freedom, that's when these ladies up in Evanston saw their golden opportunity. They got their temperance issue put on the ballot. Now, this was no accident, the timing of this issue, it was a cleverly maneuvered strategy. Taking advantage of our boys—all our young men, millions of 'em—being overseas fighting for our country and not being around to vote, like me.

That's how it happened. With all the fighting men gone, that was when the ladies of Evanston put their tem-

114

perance issue on the ballot and finally got it passed. Now, if there had been a fair representation of public opinion, there's no way that bill would ever have gotten through.

So that's what the boys came home to. No beer, no whiskey, no alcohol of any kind. Welcome home, boys. By the way, we had a vote while you were gone.

Now, I haven't told you this yet. Y' see, I was not personally in favor of a legal ban on liquor at that time. Today, with kids tearing up their lives on alcohol and drugs, and tearing up a lot of other people's lives too, well, there are some serious issues now that did not appear before. But that's something else. The point is, I personally did not think such a law would solve the problems related to alcoholism, which, of course, history shows it didn't. But once it was law, it was law. And as a man in the government service, it was my duty to enforce the law. I may not have believed in that particular law, but I did believe in the government, and I did have a very strong sense of duty. And I was honor bound to that. And so I did my job and I did it well. Which brings me to my famous spike job.

Not everybody in the beautiful town of Evanston, Illinois, belonged to the Woman's Christian Temperance Union. Evanston was an upper-class neighborhood, always had been. Lotta money out there. Now, this man Thurmond out in Evanston did something that really got my dander up.

High school kids back in those days never had much money, not like today. Most high school kids maybe earned a few coins with an odd job, but money didn't flow like it does now. And people didn't think it was so important either, didn't put so much value on money. They did other things. Family life, picnics in the park, a day at the shore. Pitchin' horseshoes, playin' Ping Pong. Or havin' a sing-along. Or a dance at some local place. It didn't have to be fancy. People did things that didn't have to cost a lot. Or maybe cost nothin'. Most people were more naive than they are today.

Now, the reason I'm pointing all this out is because it was a little different in Evanston. Families had more money, so the kids could get more money. So it came to pass that out in well-to-do Evanston even the high school kids had money. And where there's money, there's always somebody ready to run in and grab it, conscience aside. And that's what happened in Evanston.

This man Thurmond was known to be sellin' liquor to the high school kids. And that made me mad. Same as it does today when I hear about these unconscionable rats who sell all these dangerous drugs and alcohol not only to high school kids but to little children. If I were in the government service today, I tell ya, I'd be after 'em night and day.

Well, that's what was goin' on then, too. Seems there's always somebody ready to risk other people's lives as long as there's a buck in it for them. So when I heard about this Thurmond fella out in Evanston, I made sure the case was mine. I went out there with the biggest padlock I could find. A smaller padlock would have been sufficient, I'm sure, but the idea of bolting down the place with a big government padlock appealed to me. It was sort of a symbol to other people around—the government is here, and the government is strong, and the government doesn't like what's goin' on here.

Well, my big padlock was hardly the start of it. I went out there with this injunction in my hand, and I ordered the whole family out of the house. Right there on the spot, I ordered 'em out. No warning, no courteous appointment lined up in advance. I just got there, rang the front doorbell, was greeted, stepped in, announced my purpose —

putting up the injunction and evacuating the house—and that was that. Out! Now!

I guess they thought they were just gonna be taken somewhere for a nice interrogation and then be brought back home, because they were pretty docile and they did just what I said. I had my injunction to close up the house. Now, that meant what it said, close up the house. So I got the people out, and I set about closin' up the house. And all their stuff was still inside. Their clothes, their food, their personal items, everything. Now, it was not my intention to make these people starve or freeze to death. I knew they had plenty of money to solve their immediate problems. But it was my intention to expose them for what they were involved in—breaking the law of the land and doing so with reckless disregard for the naive youth of the community.

So out they went. And in I went. With a big hammer and a supply of hefty spikes that were the biggest spikes you ever saw. Mean, like railroad spikes. And I pounded spikes around every door and window in that place. I mean I closed off every room in the house. I used up forty of those spikes. I wanted to be sure those people would be locked out of their house long enough to begin to think. I even split the inside doors, so just in case anybody managed to get in there they'd have one helluva job facing 'em to get from one room to the next. The injunction meant that the house was supposed to be closed—and not accessed at all—so it could be examined for evidence pertaining to the upcoming case. And that was my job. To ensure that the place was closed. Well, I closed it all right.

When I got through splitting the inside doors and spiking shut all the outside doors and windows, I plastered up a big sign right there in the front window of the house announcing for all the world to see just why this residence had been shut up by the United States government.

Well, it made quite a stir in that town. And not just in that town. Word got around. It made the papers all over.

The Watermelon Kid

WELL, IT'S A FUNNY thing. You think you're in a very big
city and that, of course, you don't know anybody personally
who would be involved in criminal activities. But when
you're in the service of the law, every once in a while you
get a surprise. It's happened more than once. But the
instance that was the most dangerous and the most difficult
for me was the Louis Greenberg case.

I knew this fella way back in my early business days
on the streets of Chicago. He was selling watermelons and
cantaloupe and the like. He was a young man then, an
ambitious young man, maybe nineteen, twenty. In business
for himself. But the man couldn't even sign his name. He
always made an X.

So it was years later, and now I was in the government
service, room 804. And I got a warrant on a man by the
name of Alexander Louis Greenberg. Now I wondered,
could this be the same Louie Greenberg I'd knew way back
when. It said on the warrant that this man owned the
Canadian Ace Brewery and the Twelfth Street Independent Bank. Couldn't be the same guy. Not the street vendor
who couldn't even write his own name.

Well, I took the warrant and I went out to find the
place and nab this guy, who happened to have almost the
same name as an old pal of mine. It was about midnight.
We always chose the most unlikely time to call, 'cause that
was the most likely time to catch our man.

I found the address and it was a big fancy place, be-

119

fitting a man who owned a brewery and a bank. So I rang the bell and waited. And who should come to the door but the man himself, the watermelon kid. He was dressed in his shirt and pants, but he had on slippers and one of those lounging robes over it. Some nice satiny thing. Must've been up doing business on the phone or something 'cause he wasn't in his bathrobe or anything like I had gotten him out of bed.

"Alexander Louis Greenberg?" I asked.

He nodded his head yes, a little suspicious about receiving a caller in the middle of the night.

"You the same Louie Greenberg who used to sell watermelons on the streets of Chicago way back?"

He smiled, nodding his head yes again.

"Well, I hate to tell ya this, but I have a warrant with your name on it. I'm Leon Tashjian, United States deputy marshal." I showed him my badge, my credentials, and the warrant. "I'll read it to ya, Louis," I said.

"Wait a minute," he said. "What the hell has this got to do with sellin' watermelons?"

"Oh, nothin'," I said. "I'm just kinda sorry it really turned out to be you."

He cocked his head like a bird and looked at me, frowning.

"Lee," I said. "Turk. Shoeshine." Thinking he probably never even knew my formal name.

He looked again, and a smile of recognition slowly broke across his face. "Turk!" he exclaimed. "By God."

And we shook hands and patted each other on the back like it was old home week.

"It makes my job a lot harder to have to bring in a guy I used to know," I said. "But I got no choice."

"Well, c'mon in and we'll figure this thing out," he said.

He was a very nice gentleman. Very hospitable. Even to a man who had come there to deliver a warrant for his arrest. He offered me a cup of coffee and invited me to sit down, but I just didn't feel that accepting his hospitality was the thing to do, considering the circumstances.

"C'mon, Louie," I said. "Don't make it harder."

We were both uncomfortable with the situation. We kind of laughed about it, but it wasn't because it was funny. It was awkward. After all, this man was up against some pretty stiff charges, and the results of the proceedings could seriously affect the rest of his life.

So I read him the warrant, summarizing the charges and telling him where and when he had to appear and that the bond was fifty thousand dollars.

"Fifty thousand dollars?" he asked.

"Says here," I said. And I showed him the warrant and the places where the details were filled in.

"C'mon," I said. "I've got to take you down to the Federal Building."

"Well," he said, scratching his head.

Y' know, it's funny, a habit like that. Soon as he did that I remembered, he always used to do that. Scratch his head while he thought about what he was about to say. Funny how a little habit like that stays with ya.

"I think we got no problem with that bond," he said. "I'll just give ya the money."

"Oh no, not me," I said. "I can't take the money. No way. You gotta come down to the Federal Building and go through the proper procedures."

"But if I can put up the fifty-thousand-dollar bond money, I oughta be free. Not have to go in. I've got the money."

Now, bear in mind that fifty thousand dollars was a helluva lot more then than it is now. Multiply it by at least six, more likely ten. And the man was telling me he had fifty thousand dollars *cash*.

"What do I have to do?" he asked. "I've got the money for the bond. Who do we have to see?"

Well, ordinarily it would have been out of the question. Business couldn't be done until normal business hours. I would just have taken the guy down to the Federal Building, put him in custody there for the night, and let him work out the rest of it with the proper officials in the morning.

"If I can put up the bond, I shouldn't hafta be held," he said.

Well, technically, he was right. It just had never come up before. How many guys have fifty thousand dollars cash lyin' around their house that they can put their hands on in the middle of the night? Today, considering inflation over the years, that would be close to half a million bucks.

"I think I got some rights here," he added.

So, he was playin' hardball. Okay . . . But I didn't blame him. I wouldn't wanta be locked up if I didn't have to be either. Not for five minutes.

"Tell y' what," I said. "Let me call the commissioner and see what we can do."

So I called the commissioner, who at that time was Henry C. Beitler, at his home. Remember, it was somewhere around midnight.

"I'm sorry to call you in the middle of the night, Commissioner, but I got an unusual situation on my hands, and it won't wait till morning."

"Okay," he said. "Shoot."

I told him what was transpiring, and he said, "Okay, bring him over here. To my home. But on one condition. Neither you nor I can be held responsible for the money."

Louie had no problem with that, so he went to get

dressed, and when he came back he was carryin' a briefcase. I acknowledged the briefcase with a nod, and we were
on our way. Fifty thousand bucks in a briefcase in my car
in the middle of the night on the streets of Chicago didn't
make me feel too comfortable.

We drove over to the commissioner's home on Dover
Street by Lawrence Avenue, and the commissioner came
out to escort us in.

We got inside and we went over the facts so far, and
the commissioner said, "Well, it's certainly unusual, but I
suppose we can accept the bond money." He turned to me
and said, "We'll have to document all this and get all the
properly signed papers down to the Federal Building right
away. That can't wait till morning."

All this meant was that I was gonna be up all night
taking care of the details. But I was already prepared for
that.

"Wait a minute," said Louie. "I haven't got the money
on me."

"Well, what the hell did you tell me you had it for?"
I asked. "What the hell is in the briefcase?" After all this
monkey business, I was beginning to feel jerked around.

He opened the briefcase. Empty. "I never said I had
it on me," he said. "But I can get it, in minutes. From one
of my banks. The briefcase is to put it in. When we get it."

There was this stupid moment when we all sat there
looking at each other. Louie scratched his head. "Can I
make a phone call?" he asked.

So the commissioner showed him the phone, and I
was hanging around because I wanted to hear this phone
call. He made a call. I don't know who the party was, but
he said, "Meet me at the Twelfth Street Bank. I've gotta
get fifty thousand bucks. There's a government man here
with a warrant, and I wanta put up the bond."

123

That's all there was to it.

"All set," he said. "All we have to do is go down to the Twelfth Street Independent Bank. Fella's on his way to me us."

"Any funny stuff and . . ."

"No funny stuff," he said.

So there we were runnin' all over town with this defendant in the middle of the night, diggin' up fifty thousand dollars cash to carry around and worry about. Why the hell couldn't the man just spend the night in custody and straighten this all out in the morning. Of course, by now it was almost morning.

Well, we had given the man our word that he could put up the bond right away, and if that was his right, that was his right. And, in truth, I would want the same privilege extended to me. After all, the man hadn't been proven guilty of anything yet. And might never be. And a man has pride, I could understand that.

"You go with him," the commissioner said. "It'll be all right. Just bring the money back here; we'll finish up the paperwork in the morning."

So Louie and I and the empty briefcase went down to the Twelfth Street Independent Bank. When we got there, there was a guy waitin' for us. And he had a couple policemen with him. I tell ya the truth, that made me feel a little better. A man doesn't like to admit he's ever afraid of anything, and he puts up a good brave face no matter what. But the truth is, nobody wants to be set up for foul play.

I could see why the commissioner had stayed behind and just sent me down to the bank with these guys. In case they had any foul play planned, knowing the commissioner knew what they were up to and that he had a phone, et cetera, would have cooled 'em off. If we had both gone, who would be left to tell? Just in case . . .

On closer look, the guys I had taken to be policemen were security men, obviously from the security outfit entrusted with watching over the bank. Well, that was fine with me. I was still glad they were there.

They opened up the bank and let us in. Then they stood by while Louie and his partner got the money out of the vault. Fifty thousand bucks, cold cash.

"Here it is," said Louie. "As promised." He was holding out fistfuls of money to me. Like I was supposed to count it and verify that it was all there.

"No thanks," I said. "I'm not handling the money. I'd like to watch you count it, please. But then we'll go back to the commissioner and deliver it to him. I'm not gonna be responsible for that money. Not for one minute."

So they counted it out before my eyes. Fifty thousand it was. I had never seen fifty thousand dollars cash. Nor have I since. I'd like to. If it were mine.

Anyway, they stacked the money all nice and neat in the briefcase, and Louie turned to me and said, "Okay. Let's go."

So Louie and the briefcase and I got in my car one more time, and we were off. And this pal of Louie's, he got in his car and followed us. *Now, wait just a minute*, I was thinkin'. *What the hell is goin' on here?*

Yeah, he was tailin' us all right. At first I thought maybe he'd turn a different way at the corner. Or the next corner. About that time I'd have liked to have been back on the street with nothin' to worry about but my shoeshine business.

"Who invited your friend?" I finally asked.

Louie scratched his head and smiled. He musta gotten

a kick outa my uneasiness. "My friend's not invited?" he inquired.

"What the hell for?"

"Oh, I guess he feels sorta protective about this stuff," Louie said. And he patted the briefcase.

"Oh. Yeah. Not a bad idea, I guess." *Okay,* I thought to myself, *that's probably actually a pretty good idea.*

When we got back to Commissioner Beitler's house the other car pulled up behind us, but the man just stayed inside the car. I never did know who he was. Louie didn't choose to introduce us. Maybe didn't want to implicate anyone else.

The commissioner was ready for us. He had the appropriate papers all drawn up. He asked Louie to count out the money, which Louie did one more time. The man may not have been able to sign his name, but he sure could count.

"Okay," the commissioner said. "Here are the terms. I agree you have the money here to pay the bond in full. This paper, that we will both sign, verifies that. Now, I'm going to let the deputy marshal release you. But he's going to pick you up again if you don't come in tomorrow morning to my office in the Federal Building and sign some additional papers. In the meantime neither the deputy marshal nor I will be responsible for the fifty thousand dollars. I will certainly take every reasonable precaution to safeguard it, but you must understand, I cannot be held responsible for it."

Of course. Louie could have had his guys stage a house robbery or apprehend the commissioner on his way down to the Federal Building, and—what a mess we would have had then. So the commissioner was protecting himself and me the best he could.

"Now, if you want to accept those terms and sign this

paper to that effect, okay. Otherwise, if you prefer, the deputy marshal can still take you into custody, just till morning."

"It's fine," Louie said. "I trust ya."

Now, for some reason that struck me as awful funny. *He trusts us! Well now, isn't that nice.* I had to bite my lip to keep from laughing. I knew better than to mess with a man's pride.

I could see the commissioner had almost laughed too, but he didn't. "You're free to go then, Mr. Greenberg," he said instead.

The commissioner extended his hand and they shook. Then Louie turned to me and reached out his hand.

"Sorry, Louie," I said.

"Business is business," he said. And he shook my hand and smiled.

Now, how do you think that made me feel, turning in an old pal from the early days?

Louie turned and left, but he stopped in the doorway and looked back and smiled. I tried to smile politely, but I probably looked more like I was gonna be sick.

Next morning Louie was waiting for us on the front steps of the Federal Building. All dressed up in a nice lookin' three-piece suit. A very gentlemanly man. We went up to the eighth floor, signed all the proper papers, and the man was free till his court date. And you know what? He beat the rap.

I never saw him again. But I never forgot those few hours I spent with him. My life was on the line several times that night, but that was the way things went in my line of business. You got used to that; you expected it. But you never got used to the idea of delivering a federal warrant on an old pal.

The Kiss of Death

AND THEN MY OWN plunge began—but I didn't know it. A web of events was closing in on me that would strangle my career and alter my life.

Now, this was toward the end of 1926, and in the city of Chicago in those days there were a lot of hoodlums trying to elbow in on the booze business. As long as their business was basically small time, Al Capone didn't bother to boot them out. If they tried to get their foot into the big man's territory that was a different story.

Now, two of the guys who were small potatoes but big show-offs and attracted a certain amount of publicity for themselves were Terry Druggan and Frankie Lake. Everybody knew they were operating in violation of the Volstead Act, but getting the goods on 'em wasn't as easy as it seemed. Finally we got 'em, along with Peter M. Hoffman, the former sheriff. Got 'em on the Volstead Act.

It wasn't my case to bring 'em in, but after they were apprehended and the United States Grand Jury had indicted them so that they had to stand trial, I was assigned to be bodyguard to Terry Druggan and my partner, Eric Glasser, was assigned to Frankie Lake.

Our job was to keep a close eye on these guys while they awaited trial and then during the trial. We had to keep other people away from 'em and make sure they didn't pull any funny stuff. There were guys who would have liked to get to 'em, y' know. Keep 'em from talking.

So we were always there. Every minute. Never let 'em

out of our sight. We had to escort these hoodlums from the county jail where they were being held, to the Federal Building where the court proceedings were taking place, and then back to room 804. A United States deputy marshal would return them to the jail each day; that part we didn't have to worry about.

Now these guys had made quite a deal. Looking back I hafta suppose that it fits into the whole picture, although I can't say I ever had proof of who was involved or exactly how. But here's what happened.

Officially, they were being incarcerated in the Cook County jail. But they could go out every night. And they did. They'd go out for dinner, in the company of ladies, and they'd go out on the town. And then they'd be back at the jail for check in at certain times during the day. And that was all they had to do. The deal didn't smell right to me. But it wasn't my job to question things that weren't related to my responsibility, so I just had to look the other way.

We did our job and we did it very diligently. Even though these guys were sort of slick and unsavory, we got to know 'em fairly well, and we talked and even got to kiddin' around with 'em a little bit. It was part of the job, y' might say.

Now, the man who was the acting prosecutor at the trial was a man named Hope Thompson, who was a United States district attorney with big ideas about getting to be a federal judge. And he was hatching a plan that he figured would get him there. Unknown to me, I was right at the center of his plan.

Y' see, I was in the papers a lot around that time. The papers liked to make a big splash about my exploits. Partly because, at a scrawny hundred and twenty pounds, I was a featherweight up against the big gangsters of the time.

That—together with my bantam rooster courage—well, it made good press. And it gave the office a popular hero they could promote, so they could show the public that the government was tracking down these lawbreakers and closing in on 'em.

And Mr. Thompson, well, he figured out a way he could use all this to his own advantage. To help his political career. He was the kind of man who didn't think twice about destroying other people to get what he wanted. Just stepped on people like they were stepping stones across a brook. Pushed some of 'em under as he went. That was the kind of man he was.

Now, in the trial of the notorious Terry Druggan, Frankie Lake, and Peter Hoffman, a surprising verdict came down from Judge Lewis Fitzhenry. The trial had gotten a lot of publicity. The press had seized on the idea of using it as an example—let's show the booze bandits in this town that they can't get away with disregarding the law of the land. That they had better not mess with the federal government.

Everybody knew these guys were guilty. And even though it seemed like there was no doubt about the outcome of the trial, the people were grabbing up newspapers by the fistful the minute they hit the stands. They followed every development in the case. And then the verdict came down—all three of these jerks were acquitted!

Now, the papers were hotter than ever. Everybody wanted to know what was behind the acquittal. Why the case had fallen through. Who was saying what about it. It was a big case all right.

Now, on the day the verdict came down and these hoodlums were acquitted, you can bet they were pretty damn happy about it—they'd just gotten away with murder! So now that they were acquitted, they were free. As far as we were concerned, we were through with 'em. And glad of it.

Well I was out in the hall waitin' to take the elevator from the fifth floor up to the eighth and along came Terry Druggan, flyin' outa nowhere, and he tackled me! I saw him come flyin' at me, and the thought ran through my head that he'd gone crazy, with the pressure bein' off for the first time in so long.

So there I was, mindin' my own business, and all of a sudden Terry Druggan was on top o' me, *kissin'* me! I mean *kissin'* me! Not just once! Two times, three times! Callin' out how happy he was that he'd been acquitted!

"Jesus Christ!" I hollered. "Get the hell outa here!" And I punched him good to get him offa me. We wrestled a little and I let him have a coupla good punches, one especially that landed solid to his jaw. All this was goin' on in the hall by the elevator, right there in the Federal Building.

Well, I got him offa me, gave him hell, and stormed up to the eighth floor, and I told my boss, Hal Carr, about the stupid thing Terry Druggan had just done. Hittin' me with a flyin' tackle and *kissin'* me in the hall! And y' know, we really didn't think much about it at the time. We didn't see the implications in it. Not till later.

Now, in the morning along came two of my acquaintances in the federal service, Patrick Roach, who was a United States Secret Service agent, and one of his assistants, a fella by the name of Converse. For us deputy marshals, some of those federal guys never did have first names.

They were comin' up to my door, about eight o'clock in the morning. I was leaving to report to work. And there were Converse and Roach comin' up my front walk.

"Hi, Lee," said Roach.

131

"Pat, Converse. Hi. What's up?"

"We need to talk to you," Roach replied.

"Sure," I said. "Here? Y' wanta come inside?"

Roach reached into his breast pocket. "Nah," he said. "We got a warrant for your arrest."

I laughed. And then I saw he had a warrant. And he wasn't laughin'.

"What the hell . . .?"

"Sorry, Lee," Roach said.

"You're outa yer mind! What the hell is this for?"

"Bribing the jury in the Druggan-Lake case," Roach replied.

Now, I'm not a man who is often left speechless. Never have been. But I was paralyzed. Everything about the last few weeks went racin' through my head. I was tryin' to find the piece that would make this make sense. But damned if I could find it.

"C'mon," Roach said. "We gotta take you in."

Now, that was a twist. It was my job to take guys in. Guys who brashly flew in the face of the law; guys who had no regard for the rights and lives of others. And there were my own colleagues, wantin' to take *me* in! *When do I wake up from this?* I thought.

They didn't even take me in a car or on a bus, they started walkin' me. One on each side. By God, it was like they thought I was gonna pull somethin'. First time—the only time—I got a taste of how it felt to be in that position.

We walked and we walked. And we kept on walkin'. "Where the hell are we goin'?" I finally asked.

"Commonwealth Hotel," Roach replied.

"On Diversy Avenue?"

They nodded.

"Christ, that's nearly ten miles."

They nodded.

When we got there, we went up to the eighth floor and they put me in a room. And pretty soon they brought in Joe Plunkett, the son of Captain Joe Plunkett. He was accused of participating in the same alleged incident. We were left in the same room, but I have to tell you, we didn't speak a single word to each other. What was there to say?

And then a man came out of the bathroom. Turned out he had recording equipment. Was s'posed to record our conversation, but there had been no conversation to record. He thought his equipment was bad!

Converse and Roach returned. "C'mon, we're goin' to the Federal Building," they announced.

Once there, they took me to a federal judge. The judge listened to the accusations presented in brief and released me on my own recognizance. That was the first sign of humanness I had seen in a while.

When the evening papers came out, there it was in blazing headlines: "DEPUTY TRIED TO FIX JURY," "U.S. DEPUTY IS GRILLED ON JURY PICKING," "TWO IN CUSTODY AS U.S. STARTS PROBE OF HOFFMAN ACQUITTAL," "U.S. MARSHAL HELD IN HOFFMAN INQUIRY—LEON TASHJIAN ACCUSED BY FEDERAL OFFICIALS OF TAMPERING WITH PANEL."

Next came a letter from the higher ups in room 804. It read: "Sir: Because of the charges of misfeasance in your conduct as a deputy United States marshal, you have been suspended from office, said suspension taking effect with the close of business January 2, 1927. Very truly yours, Palmer E. Anderson, United States marshal."

Dated January 4, 1927, the letter informed me that I had been suspended from the federal service as of two days before. The accusations printed in the newspapers had come out in the previous two days, on January 3 and 4. Nobody had even taken time to breathe. Let alone explore the evidence or give me a chance to speak for myself. I was stunned.

Where did all this come from? I asked myself. *What went wrong? What is Hope Thompson basing his accusations on?* Well, soon enough it all came out, and the pieces of the puzzle began to fit together. And they made an ugly picture. Very ugly.

Tracking it back, it finally became clear what Mr. Hope Thompson had done. First, he had made up his mind to use this highly publicized trial of Terry Druggan and Frankie Lake to promote his own political ambition which was to become a United States federal judge. Second, he had decided that his method would be to topple the popular hero—United States Deputy Marshal Leon Tashjian. Then he had to find an angle. What could he get me on?

Thompson watched. He watched everything about that trial. And he must've had others watchin' for him, too. Because in the end he used something that almost no one could've seen. Something that happened quickly, in the hallway of the Federal Building, on the day the verdict was delivered.

Like I said, my partner, Eric, and I had been escorting Terry Druggan and Frankie Lake to and from the court proceedings every day. You got to know somebody that way. You either carried on some conversations with 'em, or you went nuts. Even if you didn't like the guy, you could be civil. So there was some small illusion of friendship among the four of us. Meant nothin' to me. Just a matter of bein' polite, since we had to live with these guys over some period of time.

Now one of the suspicious things is that when Terry Druggan came flyin' at me in the hall after the acquittal, almost nobody saw it happen. Which makes me believe to this day that the whole thing was a setup. They used it to suggest that this nut was thanking me, that he was grateful to me for helping get him off. That's where the jury-bribing thing fit in.

Thompson himself was quoted in the papers as saying, "I believe this jury was fixed. The government presented evidence that they thought, and that the presiding judge thought, was conclusive evidence of guilt. And they were confident of conviction. . . ."

Well, hell, so was I. Where did they get off putting me on the other side? But they did.

Thompson went on to say, "Almost every branch of the prosecuting force of the government of Chicago has been engaged in the inquiries. . . . Special Intelligence Unit . . . " et cetera. Oh it was a big case all right. Sensational case. The case against me was a bigger scandal than the one against Terry Druggan and Frankie Lake.

That says it all. Mr. Hope Thompson had put a warp in the Terry Druggan–Frankie Lake case, passing over the hoods who everybody knew were guilty and pointing a finger at me—the people's hero—making me look like a criminal!

If Thompson could bring me down, if he could fell the people's hero—a United States government representative who had come to stand for courage and justice in the face of intimidating odds—if he could make it look like I had been a false hero—a man subject to corruption, soliciting payoffs from gangsters, and betraying my sacred government responsibilities—what a hero he would be! The biggest hero is the one who exposes another hero as a fraud.

That was Thompson's method. And it worked. I was out. And he got in.

After it was all over, Tom Smith, who had issued the order for my arrest, called me in and apologized. "Lee,"

135

he said, "I'm sorry. I'm sorry for the whole damn thing. I've known you for so long, and you've racked up one helluva record. I was pressured by Roach and Converse, by the Intelligence guys."

It was a long row to hoe for me. There was a lengthy, drawn-out legal proceeding that cost a lot of money. I had a wife and two little girls to support, and my job had been ripped out from under me.

The papers carried the story for a long time. They printed all the accusations. But they didn't have all the facts. Finally, in the United States District Court for the Northern District of Illinois, Eastern Division, on Wednesday, October 3, 1928 (nearly two years later), the Honorable Fred L. Wamm, federal judge presiding, the case of *United States* vs. *Leon Tashjian* was dismissed on the grounds of insufficient evidence. But too much damage had been done already to ever be undone.

The newspapers were fair. They ran my acquittal with just as much hoopla as they had run the accusations. But you can't turn back the river. United States Attorney General Mabel Wildebrant, the only woman United States attorney general I know of, personally evaluated the case and considered the questionable evidence. I was told that she was the one who personally recommended the case be dropped and that she said the case never should have been taken seriously in the first place.

I was called into room 804. "We want to reinstate you," they said. "We're really sorry all this happened. Especially with your outstanding record of performance in the service. Come back."

I thought about it. I couldn't sleep kicking it all around in my head. I went in the next day and said, "Okay, I'll be reinstated."

They reinstated me. That officially cleared the record. A few days later I resigned.

I was in and out of local politics after that, but the scandal had tarnished my image in the minds of the people. The day of the Hawk had come and gone.